# MAO TSE-TUNG

## ON
## PROTRACTED WAR

University Press of the Pacific
Honolulu, Hawaii

Mao Tse-Tung
on Proctrated War

by
Mao Tse-Tung

ISBN 0-89875-179-9

Reprinted form the 1967 third edition

University Press of the Pacific
Honolulu, Hawaii
http://www.UniversityPressofthePacific.com

This series of lectures was delivered by Comrade Mao Tse-tung from May 26 to June 3, 1938, at the Yenan Association for the Study of the War of Resistance Against Japan.

Committee for the Publication of the Selected Works of Mao Tse-tung, Central Committee of the Communist Party of China

# CONTENTS

# STATEMENT OF THE PROBLEM

1. It will soon be July 7, the first anniversary of the great War of Resistance Against Japan. Rallying in unity, persevering in resistance and persevering in the united front, the forces of the whole nation have been valiantly fighting the enemy for almost a year. The people of the whole world are attentively following this war, which has no precedent in the history of the East, and which will go down as a great war in world history too. Every Chinese suffering from the disasters of the war and fighting for the survival of his nation daily yearns for victory. But what actually will be the course of the war? Can we win? Can we win quickly? Many people are talking about a protracted war, but why is it a protracted war? How to carry on a protracted war? Many people are talking about final victory, but why will final victory be ours? How shall we strive for final victory? Not everyone has found answers to these questions; in fact, to this day most people have not done so. Therefore the defeatist exponents of the theory of national subjugation have come forward to tell people that China will be subjugated, that final victory will not be China's. On the other hand, some impetuous friends have come forward to tell people that China will win very quickly without having to exert any great effort. But are these views correct? We have said all along they are not. However, most people have not yet grasped what we have been saying. This is partly because we did not do enough propaganda and explanatory work, and partly because the

development of objective events had not yet fully and clearly revealed their inherent nature and their features to the people, who were thus not in a position to foresee the over-all trend and the outcome and hence to decide on a complete set of policies and tactics. Now things are better; the experience of ten months of war has been quite sufficient to explode the utterly baseless theory of national subjugation and to dissuade our impetuous friends from their theory of quick victory. In these circumstances many people are asking for a comprehensive explanation. All the more so with regard to protracted war, not only because of the opposing theories of national subjugation and quick victory but also because of the shallow understanding of its nature. "Our four hundred million people have been making a concerted effort since the Lukouchiao Incident, and the final victory will belong to China." This formula has a wide currency. It is a correct formula but needs to be given more content. Our perseverance in the War of Resistance and in the united front has been possible because of many factors. Internally, they comprise all the political parties in the country from the Communist Party to the Kuomintang, all the people from the workers and peasants to the bourgeoisie, and all the armed forces from the regular forces to the guerrillas; internationally, they range from the land of socialism to justice-loving people in all countries; in the camp of the enemy, they range from those people in Japan who are against the war to those Japanese soldiers at the front who are against the war. In short, all these forces have contributed in varying degrees to our War of Resistance. Every man with a conscience should salute them. We Communists, together with all the other anti-Japanese political parties and the whole people, have no other course than to strive to unite all forces for the defeat of the diabolical Japanese aggressors. July 1 this year will be the 17th anniversary of the founding of the Communist Party of China. A serious study of protracted war is necessary in order to enable every Communist to play a better and greater part in the War of Resistance. Therefore my lectures will be devoted to such a study. I shall try to speak on all the problems relevant to the protracted war, but I cannot possibly go into everything in one series of lectures.

2. All the experience of the ten months of war proves the error both of the theory of China's inevitable subjugation and of the theory of China's quick victory. The former gives rise to the tendency to compromise and the latter to the tendency to underestimate the enemy. Both approaches to the problem are subjective and one-sided, or, in a word, unscientific.

3. Before the War of Resistance, there was a great deal of talk about national subjugation. Some said, "China is inferior in arms and is bound to lose in a war." Others said, "If China offers armed resistance, she is sure to become another Abyssinia." Since the beginning of the war, open talk of national subjugation has disappeared, but secret talk, and quite a lot of it too, still continues. For instance, from time to time an atmosphere of compromise arises and the advocates of compromise argue that "the continuance of the war spells subjugation".[1] In a letter from Hunan a student has written:

In the countryside everything seems difficult. Doing propaganda work on my own, I have to talk to people when and where I find them. The people I have talked to are by no means ignoramuses; they all have some understanding of what is going on and are very interested in what I have to say. But when I run into my own relatives, they always say: "China cannot win; she is doomed." They make one sick! Fortunately, they do not go around spreading their views, otherwise things would really be bad. The peasants would naturally put more stock in what they say.

Such exponents of the theory of China's inevitable subjugation form the social basis of the tendency to compromise. They are to be found everywhere in China, and therefore the problem of compromise is liable to crop up within the anti-Japanese front at any time and will probably remain with us right until the end of the war. Now that Hsuchow has fallen and Wuhan is in danger, it will not be unprofitable, I think, to knock the bottom out of the theory of national subjugation.

4. During these ten months of war all kinds of views which are indicative of impetuosity have also appeared. For instance, at the outset of the war many people were groundlessly optimistic, underestimating Japan and even believing that the Japanese could not get as far as Shansi. Some belittled the strategic role of guerrilla warfare in the War of Resistance and doubted the proposition, "With regard to the whole, mobile warfare is primary and guerrilla warfare supplementary; with regard to the parts, guerrilla warfare is primary and mobile warfare supplementary." They disagreed with the Eighth Route Army's strategy, "Guerrilla warfare is basic, but lose no chance for mobile warfare under favourable conditions", which they regarded as a "mechanical" approach.[2] During the battle of Shanghai some people said: "If we can fight for just three months, the international situation is bound to change, the Soviet Union is bound to

4

send troops, and the war will be over." They pinned their hopes for the future of the War of Resistance chiefly on foreign aid.[3] After the Taierhchuang victory,[4] some people maintained that the Hsuchow campaign should be fought as a "quasi-decisive campaign" and that the policy of protracted war should be changed. They said such things as, "This campaign marks the last desperate struggle of the enemy," or, "If we win, the Japanese warlords will be demoralized and able only to await their Day of Judgement."[5] The victory at Pinghsingkuan turned some people's heads, and further victory at Taierhchuang has turned more people's heads. Doubts have arisen as to whether the enemy will attack Wuhan. Many people think "probably not", and many others "definitely not". Such doubts may affect all major issues. For instance, is our anti-Japanese strength already sufficient? Some people may answer affirmatively, for our present strength is already sufficient to check the enemy's advance, so why increase it? Or, for instance, is the slogan "Consolidate and expand the Anti-Japanese National United Front" still correct? Some people may answer negatively, for the united front in its present state is already strong enough to repulse the enemy, so why consolidate and expand it? Or, for instance, should our efforts in diplomacy and international propaganda be intensified? Here again the answer may be in the negative. Or, for instance, should we proceed in earnest to reform the army system and the system of government, develop the mass movement, enforce education for national defence, suppress traitors and Trotskyites, develop war industries and improve the people's livelihood? Or, for instance, are the slogans calling for the defence of Wuhan, of Canton and of the Northwest and for the vigorous development of guerrilla warfare in the enemy's rear still correct? The answers might all be in the negative. There are even some people who, the moment a slightly favourable turn occurs in the war situation, are prepared to intensify the "friction" between the Kuomintang and the Communist Party, diverting attention from external to internal matters. This almost invariably occurs whenever a comparatively big battle is won or the enemy's advance comes to a temporary halt. All the above can be termed political and military short-sightedness. Such talk, however plausible, is actually specious and groundless. To sweep away such verbiage should help the victorious prosecution of the War of Resistance.

5. The question now is: Will China be subjugated? The answer is, No, she will not be subjugated, but will win final victory. Can China win quickly? The answer is, No, she cannot win quickly, and the War of Resistance will be a protracted war.

6. As early as two years ago, we broadly indicated the main arguments on these questions. On July 16, 1936, five months before the Sian Incident and twelve months before the Lukouchiao Incident, in an interview with the American correspondent, Mr. Edgar Snow, I made a general estimate of the situation with regard to war between China and Japan and advanced various principles for winning victory. The following excerpts may serve as a reminder:

*Question:* Under what conditions do you think China can defeat and destroy the forces of Japan?

*Answer:* Three conditions are required: first, the establishment of an anti-Japanese united front in China; second, the formation of an international anti-Japanese united front; third, the rise of the revolutionary movement of the people in Japan and the Japanese colonies. From the standpoint of the Chinese people, the unity of the people of China is the most important of the three conditions.

*Question:* How long do you think such a war would last?

*Answer:* That depends on the strength of China's anti-Japanese united front and many other conditioning factors involving China and Japan. That is to say, apart from China's own strength, which is the main thing, international help to China and the help rendered by the revolution in Japan are also important. If China's anti-Japanese united front is greatly expanded and effectively organized horizontally and vertically, if the necessary help is given to China by those governments and peoples which recognize the Japanese imperialist menace to their own interests and if revolution comes quickly in Japan, the war will speedily be brought to an end and China will speedily win victory. If these conditions are not realized quickly, the war will be prolonged. But in the end, just the same, Japan will certainly be defeated and China will certainly be victorious. Only the sacrifices will be great and there will be a very painful period.

*Question:* What is your opinion of the probable course of development of such a war, politically and militarily?

*Answer:* Japan's continental policy is already fixed, and those who think they can halt the Japanese advance by making compromises with Japan at the expense of more Chinese territory and sovereign rights are indulging in mere fantasy. We definitely know that the lower Yangtse valley and our southern seaports are already included in the continental programme of Japanese imperialism.

Moreover, Japan wants to occupy the Philippines, Siam, Indo-China, the Malay Peninsula and the Dutch East Indies in order to cut off other countries from China and monopolize the southwestern Pacific. This is Japan's maritime policy. In such a period, China will undoubtedly be in an extremely difficult position. But the majority of the Chinese people believe that such difficulties can be overcome; only the rich in the big port cities are defeatists because they are afraid of losing their property. Many people think it would be impossible for China to continue the war, once her coastline is blockaded by Japan. This is nonsense. To refute them we need only cite the war history of the Red Army. In the present War of Resistance Against Japan, China's position is much superior to that of the Red Army in the civil war. China is a vast country, and even if Japan should succeed in occupying a section of China with as many as 100 to 200 million people, we would still be far from defeated. We would still have ample strength to fight against Japan, while the Japanese would have to fight defensive battles in their rear throughout the war. The heterogeneity and uneven development of China's economy are rather advantageous in the war of resistance. For example, to sever Shanghai from the rest of China would definitely not be as disastrous to China as would be the severance of New York from the rest of the United States. Even if Japan blockades the Chinese coastline, it is impossible for her to blockade China's Northwest, Southwest and West. Thus, once more the central point of the problem is the unity of the entire Chinese people and the building up of a nation-wide anti-Japanese front. This is what we have long been advocating.

8

*Question:* If the war drags on for a long time and Japan is not completely defeated, would the Communist Party agree to the negotiation of a peace with Japan and recognize her rule in northeastern China?

*Answer:* No. Like the people of the whole country, the Chinese Communist Party will not allow Japan to retain an inch of Chinese territory.

*Question:* What, in your opinion, should be the main strategy and tactics to be followed in this "war of liberation"?

*Answer:* Our strategy should be to employ our main forces to operate over an extended and fluid front. To achieve success, the Chinese troops must conduct their warfare with a high degree of mobility on extensive battlefields, making swift advances and withdrawals, swift concentrations and dispersals. This means large-scale mobile warfare, and not positional warfare depending exclusively on defence works with deep trenches, high fortresses and successive rows of defensive positions. It does not mean the abandonment of all the vital strategic points, which should be defended by positional warfare as long as profitable. But the pivotal strategy must be mobile warfare. Positional warfare is also necessary, but strategically it is auxiliary and secondary. Geographically the theatre of the war is so vast that it is possible for us to conduct mobile warfare most effectively. In the face of the vigorous actions of our forces, the Japanese army will have to be cautious. Its war-machine is ponderous and slow-moving, with limited efficiency. If we concentrate our forces on a narrow front for a defensive war of attrition, we would be throwing away the advantages of our

9

geography and economic organization and repeating the mistake of Abyssinia. In the early period of the war, we must avoid any major decisive battles, and must first employ mobile warfare gradually to break the morale and combat effectiveness of the enemy troops.

Besides employing trained armies to carry on mobile warfare, we must organize great numbers of guerrilla units among the peasants. One should know that the anti-Japanese volunteer units in the three northeastern provinces are only a minor demonstration of the latent power of resistance that can be mobilized from the peasants of the whole country. The Chinese peasants have very great latent power; properly organized and directed, they can keep the Japanese army busy twenty-four hours a day and worry it to death. It must be remembered that the war will be fought in China, that is to say, the Japanese army will be entirely surrounded by the hostile Chinese people, it will be forced to move in all its provisions and guard them, it must use large numbers of troops to protect its lines of communications and constantly guard against attacks, and it needs large forces to garrison Manchuria and Japan as well.

In the course of the war, China will be able to capture many Japanese soldiers and seize many weapons and munitions with which to arm herself; at the same time China will win foreign aid to reinforce the equipment of her troops gradually. Therefore China will be able to conduct positional warfare in the latter period of the war and make positional attacks on the Japanese-occupied areas. Thus Japan's economy will crack under the strain of China's long resistance and the morale of the Japanese forces will break under the trial of innumerable battles. On the Chinese side, however, the growing latent power of resistance will be constantly brought into play and large numbers of revolutionary people will be pouring into the front lines to fight for their freedom. The combination of all these and other factors will enable us to make the final and decisive attacks on the fortifications and bases in the Japanese-occupied areas and drive the Japanese forces of aggression out of China.

The above views have been proved correct in the light of the experience of the ten months of war and will also be borne out in the future.

7. As far back as August 25, 1937, less than two months after the Lukouchiao Incident, the Central Committee of the Chinese Communist Party clearly pointed out in its "Resolution on the Present Situation and the Tasks of the Party":

The military provocation by the Japanese aggressors at Lukouchiao and their occupation of Peiping and Tientsin represent only the beginning of their large-scale invasion of China south of the Great Wall. They have already begun their national mobilization for war. Their propaganda that they have "no desire to aggravate the situation" is only a smokescreen for further attacks.

The resistance at Lukouchiao on July 7 marked the starting point of China's national War of Resistance.

Thus a new stage has opened in China's political situation, the stage of actual resistance. The stage of preparation for resistance is over. In the present stage the central task is to mobilize all the nation's forces for victory in the War of Resistance.

The key to victory in the war now lies in developing the resistance that has already begun into a war of total resistance by the whole nation. Only through such a war of total resistance can final victory be won.

The existence of serious weaknesses in the War of Resistance may lead to many setbacks, retreats, internal splits, betrayals, temporary and partial compromises and other such reverses. Therefore it should be realized that the war will be an arduous and protracted war. But we are confident that, through the efforts of our Party and the whole people, the resistance already started will sweep aside all obstacles and continue to advance and develop.

The above thesis, too, has been proved correct in the light of the experience of the ten months of war and will also be borne out in the future.

8. Epistemologically speaking, the source of all erroneous views on war lies in idealist and mechanistic tendencies on the question. People with such tendencies are subjective and one-sided in their approach to problems. They either indulge in groundless and purely subjective talk, or, basing themselves upon a single aspect or a temporary manifestation, magnify it with similar subjectivity into the whole of the problem. But there are two categories of erroneous views, one comprising fundamental, and therefore consistent, errors which are hard to correct, and the other comprising accidental, and therefore temporary, errors which are easy to correct. Since both are wrong, both need to be corrected. Therefore, only by opposing idealist and mechanistic tendencies and taking an objective and all-sided view in making a study of war can we draw correct conclusions on the question of war.

## THE BASIS OF THE PROBLEM

9. Why is the War of Resistance Against Japan a protracted war? Why will the final victory be China's? What is the basis for these statements?

The war between China and Japan is not just any war, it is specifically a war of life and death between semi-colonial and semi-feudal China and imperialist Japan, fought in the Nineteen Thirties. Herein lies the basis of the whole problem. The two sides in the war have many contrasting features, which will be considered in turn below.

10. *The Japanese side.* First, Japan is a powerful imperialist country, which ranks first in the East in military, economic and political-organizational power, and is one of the five or six foremost imperialist countries of the world. These are the basic factors in Japan's war of aggression. The inevitability of the war and the impossibility of quick victory for China are due to Japan's imperialist system and her great military, economic and political-organizational power. Secondly, however, the imperialist character of Japan's social economy determines the imperialist character of her war, a war that is retrogressive and barbarous. In the Nineteen Thirties, the internal and external contradictions of Japanese imperialism have driven her not only to embark on an adventurist war unparalleled in scale but also to approach her final collapse. In terms of social development, Japan is no longer a thriving country; the war will not lead to the prosperity sought by her ruling classes but to the very reverse, the doom of Japanese imperialism. This is what we mean by the retrogressive nature of Japan's war. It is this reactionary quality, coupled with the military-feudal character of Japanese imperialism, that gives rise to the

peculiar barbarity of Japan's war. All of which will arouse to the utmost the class antagonisms within Japan, the antagonism between the Japanese and the Chinese nations, and the antagonism between Japan and most other countries of the world. The reactionary and barbarous character of Japan's war constitutes the primary reason for her inevitable defeat. Thirdly, Japan's war is conducted on the basis of her great military, economic and political-organizational power, but at the same time it rests on an inadequate natural endowment. Japan's military, economic and political-organizational power is great but quantitatively inadequate. Japan is a comparatively small country, deficient in manpower and in military, financial and material resources, and she cannot stand a long war. Japan's rulers are endeavouring to resolve this difficulty through war, but again they will get the very reverse of what they desire; that is to say, the war they have launched to resolve this difficulty will eventually aggravate it and even exhaust Japan's original resources. Fourthly and lastly, while Japan can get international support from the fascist countries, the international opposition she is bound to encounter will be greater than her international support. This opposition will gradually grow and eventually not only cancel out the support but even bear down upon Japan herself. Such is the law that an unjust cause finds meagre support, and such is the consequence of the very nature of Japan's war. To sum up, Japan's advantage lies in her great capacity to wage war, and her disadvantages lie in the reactionary and barbarous nature of her war, in the inadequacy of her manpower and material resources, and in her meagre international support. These are the characteristics on the Japanese side.

11. *The Chinese side.* First, we are a semi-colonial and semi-feudal country. The Opium War,[6] the Taiping Revolution,[7] the Reform Movement of 1898,[8] the Revolution of 1911[9] and the Northern Expedition[10] — the revolutionary or reform movements which aimed at extricating China from her semi-colonial and semi-feudal state — all met with serious setbacks, and China remains a semi-colonial and semi-feudal country. We are still a weak country and manifestly inferior to the enemy in military, economic and political-organizational power. Here again one can find the basis for the inevitability of the war and the impossibility of quick victory for China. Secondly, however, China's liberation movement, with its cumulative development over the last hundred years, is now different from that of any previous period. Although the domestic and foreign forces opposing it have caused it serious setbacks, at the same time they have tempered the Chinese people. Although China today is not so strong as Japan militarily, economically, politically and culturally, yet there are factors in China more progressive than in any other period of her history. The Communist Party of China and the army under its leadership represent these progressive factors. It is on the basis of this progress that China's present war of liberation can be protracted and can achieve final victory. By contrast with Japanese imperialism, which is declining, China is a country rising like the morning sun. China's war is progressive, hence its just character. Because it is a just war, it is capable of arousing the nation to unity, of evoking the sympathy of the people in Japan and of winning the support of most countries in the world. Thirdly, and again by contrast with Japan, China is a very big country with vast territory, rich resources, a large population and plenty of soldiers, and is capable of sustaining a long war.

Fourthly and lastly, there is broad international support for China stemming from the progressive and just character of her war, which is again exactly the reverse of the meagre support for Japan's unjust cause. To sum up, China's disadvantage lies in her military weakness, and her advantages lie in the progressive and just character of her war, her great size and her abundant international support. These are China's characteristics.

12. Thus it can be seen that Japan has great military, economic and political-organizational power, but that her war is reactionary and barbarous, her manpower and material resources are inadequate, and she is in an unfavourable position internationally. China, on the contrary, has less military, economic and political-organizational power, but she is in her era of progress, her war is progressive and just, she is moreover a big country, a factor which enables her to sustain a protracted war, and she will be supported by most countries. The above are the basic, mutually contradictory characteristics of the Sino-Japanese war. They have determined and are determining all the political policies and military strategies and tactics of the two sides; they have determined and are determining the protracted character of the war and its outcome, namely, that the final victory will go to China and not to Japan. The war is a contest between these characteristics. They will change in the course of the war, each according to its own nature; and from this everything else will follow. These characteristics exist objectively and are not invented to deceive people; they constitute all the basic elements of the war, and are not incomplete fragments; they permeate all major and minor problems on both sides and all stages of the war, and they are not matters of no consequence. If anyone forgets these characteristics in studying the Sino-

Japanese war, he will surely go wrong; and even though some of his ideas win credence for a time and may seem right, they will inevitably be proved wrong by the course of the war. On the basis of these characteristics we shall now proceed to explain the problems to be dealt with.

## REFUTATION OF THE THEORY OF NATIONAL SUBJUGATION

13. The theorists of national subjugation, who see nothing but the contrast between the enemy's strength and our weakness, used to say, "Resistance will mean subjugation," and now they are saying, "The continuance of the war spells subjugation." We shall not be able to convince them merely by stating that Japan, though strong, is small, while China, though weak, is large. They can adduce historical instances, such as the destruction of the Sung Dynasty by the Yuan and the destruction of the Ming Dynasty by the Ching, to prove that a small but strong country can vanquish a large but weak one and, moreover, that a backward country can vanquish an advanced one. If we say these events occurred long ago and do not prove the point, they can cite the British subjugation of India to prove that a small but strong capitalist country can vanquish a large but weak and backward country. Therefore, we have to produce other grounds before we can silence and convince all the subjugationists, and supply everyone engaged in propaganda with adequate arguments to persuade those who are still confused or irresolute and so strengthen their faith in the War of Resistance.

14. What then are the grounds we should advance? The characteristics of the epoch. These characteristics are

concretely reflected in Japan's retrogression and paucity of support and in China's progress and abundance of support.

15. Our war is not just any war, it is specifically a war between China and Japan fought in the Nineteen Thirties. Our enemy, Japan, is first of all a moribund imperialist power; she is already in her era of decline and is not only different from Britain at the time of the subjugation of India, when British capitalism was still in the era of its ascendency, but also different from what she herself was at the time of World War I twenty years ago. The present war was launched on the eve of the general collapse of world imperialism and, above all, of the fascist countries; that is the very reason the enemy has launched this adventurist war, which is in the nature of a last desperate struggle. Therefore, it is an inescapable certainty that it will not be China but the ruling circles of Japanese imperialism which will be destroyed as a result of the war. Moreover, Japan has undertaken this war at a time when many countries have been or are about to be embroiled in war, when we are all fighting or preparing to fight against barbarous aggression, and China's fortunes are linked with those of most of the countries and peoples of the world. This is the root cause of the opposition Japan has aroused and will increasingly arouse among those countries and peoples.

16. What about China? The China of today cannot be compared with the China of any other historical period. She is a semi-colony and a semi-feudal society, and she is consequently considered a weak country. But at the same time, China is historically in her era of progress; this is the primary reason for her ability to defeat Japan. When we say that the War of Resistance Against Japan is progressive, we do not mean progressive in the ordinary or general sense, nor do

we mean progressive in the sense that the Abyssinian war against Italy, or the Taiping Revolution or the Revolution of 1911 were progressive, we mean progressive in the sense that China is progressive today. In what way is the China of today progressive? She is progressive because she is no longer a completely feudal country and because we already have some capitalism in China, we have a bourgeoisie and a proletariat, we have vast numbers of people who have awakened or are awakening, we have a Communist Party, we have a politically progressive army — the Chinese Red Army led by the Communist Party — and we have the tradition and the experience of many decades of revolution, and especially the experience of the seventeen years since the founding of the Chinese Communist Party. This experience has schooled the people and the political parties of China and forms the very basis for the present unity against Japan. If it is said that without the experience of 1905 the victory of 1917 would have been impossible in Russia, then we can also say that without the experience of the last seventeen years it would be impossible to win our War of Resistance. Such is the internal situation.

In the existing international situation, China is not isolated in the war, and this fact too is without precedent in history. In the past, China's wars, and India's too, were wars fought in isolation. It is only today that we meet with world-wide popular movements, extraordinary in breadth and depth, which have arisen or are arising and which are supporting China. The Russian Revolution of 1917 also received international support, and thus the Russian workers and peasants won; but that support was not so broad in scale and deep in nature as ours today. The popular movements in the world today are developing on a scale and with a depth that are unprecedented. The existence of the Soviet Union is a particularly vital factor in present-day international politics, and the Soviet Union will certainly support China with the greatest enthusiasm; there was nothing like this twenty years ago. All these factors have created and are creating important conditions indispensable to China's final victory. Large-scale direct assistance is as yet lacking and will come only in the future, but China is progressive and is a big country, and these are the factors enabling her to protract the war and to promote as well as await international help.

17. There is the additional factor that while Japan is a small country with a small territory, few resources, a small population and a limited number of soldiers, China is a big country with vast territory, rich resources, a large population and plenty of soldiers, so that, besides the contrast between strength and weakness, there is the contrast between a small country, retrogression and meagre support and a big country, progress and abundant support. This is the reason why China will never be subjugated. It follows from the contrast between strength and weakness that Japan can ride rough-shod over China for a certain time and to a certain extent, that China must unavoidably travel a hard stretch of road, and that the War of Resistance will be a protracted war and not a war of quick decision; nevertheless, it follows from the other contrast — a small country, retrogression and meagre support versus a big country, progress and abundant support — that Japan cannot ride roughshod over China indefinitely but is sure to meet final defeat, while China can never be subjugated but is sure to win final victory.

18. Why was Abyssinia vanquished? First, she was not only weak but also small. Second, she was not as progressive

as China; she was an old country passing from the slave to the serf system, a country without any capitalism or bourgeois political parties, let alone a Communist Party, and with no army such as the Chinese army, let alone one like the Eighth Route Army. Third, she was unable to hold out and wait for international assistance and had to fight her war in isolation. Fourth, and most important of all, there were mistakes in the direction of her war against Italy. Therefore Abyssinia was subjugated. But there is still quite extensive guerrilla warfare in Abyssinia, which, if persisted in, will enable the Abyssinians to recover their country when the world situation changes.

19. If the subjugationists quote the history of the failure of liberation movements in modern China to prove their assertions first that "resistance will mean subjugation", and then that "the continuance of the war spells subjugation", here again our answer is, "Times are different." China herself, the internal situation in Japan and the international environment are all different now. It is a serious matter that Japan is stronger than before while China in her unchanged semi-colonial and semi-feudal position is still fairly weak. It is also a fact that for the time being Japan can still control her people at home and exploit international contradictions in order to invade China. But during a long war, these things are bound to change in the opposite direction. Such changes are not yet accomplished facts, but they will become so in future. The subjugationists dismiss this point. As for China, we already have new people, a new political party, a new army and a new policy of resistance to Japan, a situation very different from that of over a decade ago, and what is more, all these will inevitably make further progress. It is true that historically the liberation movements met with

21

repeated setbacks with the result that China could not accumulate greater strength for the present War of Resistance — this is a very painful historical lesson, and never again should we destroy any of our revolutionary forces. Yet even on the present basis, by exerting great efforts we can certainly forge ahead gradually and increase the strength of our resistance. All such efforts should converge on the great Anti-Japanese National United Front. As for international support, though direct and large-scale assistance is not yet in sight, it is in the making, the international situation being fundamentally different from before. The countless failures in the liberation movement of modern China had their subjective and objective causes, but the situation today is entirely different. Today, although there are many difficulties which make the War of Resistance arduous — such as the enemy's strength and our weakness, and the fact that his difficulties are just starting, while our own progress is far from sufficient — nevertheless many favourable conditions exist for defeating the enemy; we need only add our subjective efforts, and we shall be able to overcome the difficulties and win through to victory. These are favourable conditions such as never existed before in any period of our history, and that is why the War of Resistance Against Japan, unlike the liberation movements of the past, will not end in failure.

## COMPROMISE OR RESISTANCE?
## CORRUPTION OR PROGRESS?

20. It has been fully explained above that the theory of national subjugation is groundless. But there are many people who do not subscribe to this theory; they are honest

patriots, who are nevertheless deeply worried about the present situation. Two things are worrying them, fear of a compromise with Japan and doubts about the possibility of political progress. These two vexing questions are being widely discussed and no key has been found to their solution. Let us now examine them.

21. As previously explained, the question of compromise has its social roots, and as long as these roots exist the question is bound to arise. But compromise will not avail. To prove the point, again we need only look for substantiation to Japan, China, and the international situation. First take Japan. At the very beginning of the War of Resistance, we estimated that the time would come when an atmosphere conducive to compromise would arise, in other words, that after occupying northern China, Kiangsu and Chekiang, Japan would probably resort to the scheme of inducing China to capitulate. True enough, she did resort to the scheme, but the crisis soon passed, one reason being that the enemy everywhere pursued a barbarous policy and practised naked plunder. Had China capitulated, every Chinese would have become a slave without a country. The enemy's predatory policy, the policy of subjugating China, has two aspects, the material and the spiritual, both of which are being applied universally to all Chinese, not only to the people of the lower strata but also to members of the upper strata; of course the latter are treated a little more politely, but the difference is only one of degree, not of principle. In the main the enemy is transplanting into the interior of China the same old measures he adopted in the three northeastern provinces. Materially, he is robbing the common people even of their food and clothing, making them cry out in hunger and cold; he is plundering the means of production, thus ruining and

enslaving China's national industries. Spiritually, he is working to destroy the national consciousness of the Chinese people. Under the flag of the "Rising Sun" all Chinese are forced to be docile subjects, beasts of burden forbidden to show the slightest trace of Chinese national spirit. This barbarous enemy policy will be carried deeper into the interior of China. Japan with her voracious appetite is unwilling to stop the war. As was inevitable, the policy set forth in the Japanese cabinet's statement of January 16, 1938[11] is still being obstinately carried out, which has enraged all strata of the Chinese people. This rage is engendered by the reactionary and barbarous character of Japan's war — "there is no escape from fate", and hence an absolute hostility has crystallized. It is to be expected that on some future occasion the enemy will once again resort to the scheme of inducing China to capitulate and that certain subjugationists will again crawl out and most probably collude with certain foreign elements (to be found in Britain, the United States and France, and especially among the upper strata in Britain) as partners in crime. But the general trend of events will not permit capitulation; the obstinate and peculiarly barbarous character of Japan's war has decided this aspect of the question.

22. Second, let us take China. There are three factors contributing to China's perseverance in the War of Resistance. In the first place, the Communist Party, which is the reliable force leading the people to resist Japan. Next, the Kuomintang, which depends on Britain and the United States and hence will not capitulate to Japan unless they tell it to. Finally, the other political parties and groups, most of which oppose compromise and support the War of Resistance. With unity among these three, whoever compromises will be

standing with the traitors, and anybody will have the right to punish him. All those unwilling to be traitors have no choice but to unite and carry on the War of Resistance to the end; therefore compromise can hardly succeed.

23. Third, take the international aspect. Except for Japan's allies and certain elements in the upper strata of other capitalist countries, the whole world is in favour of resistance, and not of compromise by China. This factor reinforces China's hopes. Today the people throughout the country cherish the hope that international forces will gradually give China increasing help. It is not a vain hope; the existence of the Soviet Union in particular encourages China in her War of Resistance. The socialist Soviet Union, now strong as never before, has always shared China's joys and sorrows. In direct contrast to all the members of the upper strata in the capitalist countries who seek nothing but profits, the Soviet Union considers it its duty to help all weak nations and all revolutionary wars. That China is not fighting her war in isolation has its basis not only in international support in general but in Soviet support in particular. China and the Soviet Union are in close geographical proximity, which aggravates Japan's crisis and facilitates China's War of Resistance. Geographical proximity to Japan increases the difficulties of China's resistance. Proximity to the Soviet Union, on the other hand, is a favourable condition for the War of Resistance.

24. Hence we may conclude that the danger of compromise exists but can be overcome. Even if the enemy can modify his policy to some extent, he cannot alter it fundamentally. In China the social roots of compromise are present, but the opponents of compromise are in the majority. Internationally, also, some forces favour compromise but the

main forces favour resistance. The combination of these three factors makes it possible to overcome the danger of compromise and persist to the end in the War of Resistance.

25. Let us now answer the second question. Political progress at home and perseverance in the War of Resistance are inseparable. The greater the political progress, the more we can persevere in the war, and the more we persevere in the war, the greater the political progress. But, fundamentally, everything depends on our perseverance in the War of Resistance. The unhealthy phenomena in various fields under the Kuomintang regime are very serious, and the accumulation of these undesirable factors over the years has caused great anxiety and vexation among the broad ranks of our patriots. But there is no ground for pessimism, since experience in the War of Resistance has already proved that the Chinese people have made as much progress in the last ten months as in many years in the past. Although the cumulative effects of long years of corruption are seriously retarding the growth of the people's strength to resist Japan, thus reducing the extent of our victories and causing us losses in the war, yet the over-all situation in China, in Japan and in the world is such that the Chinese people cannot but make progress. This progress will be slow because of the factor of corruption, which impedes progress. Progress and the slow pace of progress are two characteristics of the present situation, and the second ill accords with the urgent needs of the war, which is a source of great concern to patriots. But we are in the midst of a revolutionary war, and revolutionary war is an antitoxin which not only eliminates the enemy's poison but also purges us of our own filth. Every just, revolutionary war is endowed with tremendous power, which can transform many things or clear the way for their

transformation. The Sino-Japanese war will transform both China and Japan; provided China perseveres in the War of Resistance and in the united front, the old Japan will surely be transformed into a new Japan and the old China into a new China, and people and everything else in both China and Japan will be transformed during and after the war. It is proper for us to regard the anti-Japanese war and our national reconstruction as interconnected. To say that Japan can also be transformed is to say that the war of aggression by her rulers will end in defeat and may lead to a revolution by the Japanese people. The day of triumph of the Japanese people's revolution will be the day Japan is transformed. All this is closely linked with China's War of Resistance and is a prospect we should take into account.

## THE THEORY OF NATIONAL SUBJUGATION IS WRONG AND THE THEORY OF QUICK VICTORY IS LIKEWISE WRONG

26. In our comparative study of the enemy and ourselves with respect to the basic contradictory characteristics, such as relative strength, relative size, progress or reaction, and the relative extent of support, we have already refuted the theory of national subjugation, and we have explained why compromise is unlikely and why political progress is possible. The subjugationists stress the contradiction between strength and weakness and puff it up until it becomes the basis of their whole argument on the question, neglecting all the other contradictions. Their preoccupation with the contrast in

strength shows their one-sidedness, and their exaggeration of this one side of the matter into the whole shows their subjectivism. Thus, if one looks at the matter as a whole, it will be seen that they have no ground to stand on and are wrong. As for those who are neither subjugationists nor confirmed pessimists, but who are in a pessimistic frame of mind for the moment simply because they are confused by the disparity between our strength and that of the enemy at a given time and in certain respects or by the corruption in the country, we should point out to them that their approach also tends to be one-sided and subjective. But in their case correction is relatively easy; once they are alerted, they will understand, for they are patriots and their error is only momentary.

27. The exponents of quick victory are likewise wrong. Either they completely forget the contradiction between strength and weakness, remembering only the other contradictions, or they exaggerate China's advantages beyond all semblance of reality and beyond recognition, or they presumptuously take the balance of forces at one time and place for the whole situation, as in the old saying, "A leaf before the eye shuts out Mount Tai." In a word, they lack the courage to admit that the enemy is strong while we are weak. They often deny this point and consequently deny one aspect of the truth. Nor do they have the courage to admit the limitations of our advantages, and thus they deny another aspect of the truth. The result is that they make mistakes, big and small, and here again it is subjectivism and one-sidedness that are doing the mischief. These friends have their hearts in the right place, and they, too, are patriots. But while "the gentlemen's aspirations are indeed lofty", their views are wrong, and to act according to them would

28

certainly be to run into a brick wall.  For if appraisal does not conform to reality, action cannot attain its objective; and to act notwithstanding would mean the army's defeat and the nation's subjugation, so that the result would be the same as with the defeatists.  Hence this theory of quick victory will not do either.

28. Do we deny the danger of national subjugation?  No, we do not.  We recognize that China faces two possible prospects, liberation or subjugation, and that the two are in violent conflict.  Our task is to achieve liberation and to avert subjugation.  The conditions for liberation are China's progress, which is basic, the enemy's difficulties, and international support.  We differ from the subjugationists.  Taking an objective and all-sided view, we recognize the two possibilities of national subjugation and liberation, stress that liberation is the dominant possibility, point out the conditions for its achievement, and strive to secure them.  The subjugationists, on the other hand, taking a subjective and one-sided view, recognize only one possibility, that of subjugation; they do not admit the possibility of liberation, and still less point out the conditions necessary for liberation or strive to secure them.  Moreover, while acknowledging the tendency to compromise and the corruption, we see other tendencies and phenomena which, we indicate, will gradually prevail and are already in violent conflict with the former; in addition, we point out the conditions necessary for the healthy tendencies and phenomena to prevail, and we strive to overcome the tendency to compromise and to change the state of corruption.  Therefore, contrary to the pessimists, we are not at all down-hearted.

29. Not that we would not like a quick victory; everybody would be in favour of driving the "devils" out overnight.

But we point out that, in the absence of certain definite conditions, quick victory is something that exists only in one's mind and not in objective reality, and that it is a mere illusion, a false theory. Accordingly, having made an objective and comprehensive appraisal of all the circumstances concerning both the enemy and ourselves, we point out that the only way to final victory is the strategy of protracted war, and we reject the groundless theory of quick victory. We maintain that we must strive to secure all the conditions indispensable to final victory, and the more fully and the earlier these conditions are secured, the surer we shall be of victory and the earlier we shall win it. We believe that only in this way can the course of the war be shortened, and we reject the theory of quick victory, which is just idle talk and an effort to get things on the cheap.

## WHY A PROTRACTED WAR?

30. Let us now examine the problem of protracted war. A correct answer to the question "Why a protracted war?" can be arrived at only on the basis of all the fundamental contrasts between China and Japan. For instance, if we say merely that the enemy is a strong imperialist power while we are a weak semi-colonial and ´semi-feudal country, we are in danger of falling into the theory of national subjugation. For neither in theory nor in practice can a struggle become protracted by simply pitting the weak against the strong. Nor can it become protracted by simply pitting the big against the small, the progressive against the reactionary, or abundant support against meagre support. The annexation of a small country by a big one or of a big country

by a small one is a common occurrence. It often happens that a progressive country which is not strong is destroyed by a big, reactionary country, and the same holds for everything that is progressive but not strong. Abundant or meagre support is an important but a subsidiary factor, and the degree of its effect depends upon the fundamental factors on both sides. Therefore when we say that the War of Resistance Against Japan is a protracted war, our conclusion is derived from the interrelations of all the factors at work on both sides. The enemy is strong and we are weak, and the danger of subjugation is there. But in other respects the enemy has shortcomings and we have advantages. The enemy's advantage can be reduced and his shortcomings aggravated by our efforts. On the other hand, our advantages can be enhanced and our shortcoming remedied by our efforts. Hence, we can win final victory and avert subjugation, while the enemy will ultimately be defeated and will be unable to avert the collapse of his whole imperialist system.

31. Since the enemy has advantages only in one respect but shortcomings in all others and we have shortcomings in only one respect but advantages in all others, why has this produced not a balance, but, on the contrary, a superior position for him and an inferior position for us at the present time? Quite clearly, we cannot consider the question in such a formal way. The fact is that the disparity between the enemy's strength and our own is now so great that the enemy's shortcomings have not developed, and for the time being cannot develop, to a degree sufficient to offset his strength, while our advantages have not developed, and for the time being cannot develop, to a degree sufficient to

compensate for our weakness. Therefore there can as yet be no balance, only imbalance.

32. Although our efforts in persevering in the War of Resistance and the united front have somewhat changed the enemy's strength and superiority as against our weakness and inferiority, there has as yet been no basic change. Hence during a certain stage of the war, to a certain degree the enemy will be victorious and we shall suffer defeat. But why is it that in this stage the enemy's victories and our defeats are definitely restricted in degree and cannot be transcended by complete victory or complete defeat? The reason is that, first, from the very beginning the enemy's strength and our weakness have been relative and not absolute, and that, second, our efforts in persevering in the War of Resistance and in the united front have further accentuated this relativeness. In comparison with the original situation, the enemy is still strong, but unfavourable factors have reduced his strength, although not yet to a degree sufficient to destroy his superiority, and similarly we are still weak, but favourable factors have compensated for our weakness, although not yet to a degree sufficient to transform our inferiority. Thus it turns out that the enemy is relatively strong and we are relatively weak, that the enemy is in a relatively superior and we are in a relatively inferior position. On both sides, strength and weakness, superiority and inferiority, have never been absolute, and besides, our efforts in persevering in resistance to Japan and in the united front during the war have brought about further changes in the original balance of forces between us and the enemy. Therefore, in this stage the enemy's victory and our defeat are definitely restricted in degree, and hence the war becomes protracted.

33. But circumstances are continually changing. In the course of the war, provided we employ correct military and political tactics, make no mistakes of principle and exert our best efforts, the enemy's disadvantages and China's advantages will both grow as the war is drawn out, with the inevitable result that there will be a continual change in the difference in comparative strength and hence in the relative position of the two sides. When a new stage is reached, a great change will take place in the balance of forces, resulting in the enemy's defeat and our victory.

34. At present the enemy can still manage to exploit his strength, and our War of Resistance has not yet fundamentally weakened him. The insufficiency in his manpower and material resources is not yet such as to prevent his offensive; on the contrary, they can still sustain his offensive to a certain extent. The reactionary and barbarous nature of his war, a factor which intensifies both class antagonisms within Japan and the resistance of the Chinese nation, has not yet brought about a situation which radically impedes his advance. The enemy's international isolation is increasing but is not yet complete. In many countries which have indicated they will help us, the capitalists dealing in munitions and war materials and bent solely on profit are still furnishing Japan with large quantities of war supplies,[12] and their governments[13] are still reluctant to join the Soviet Union in practical sanctions against Japan. From all this it follows that our War of Resistance cannot be won quickly and can only be a protracted war. As for China, although there has been some improvement with regard to her weakness in the military, economic, political and cultural spheres in the ten months of resistance, it is still a long way from what is required to prevent the enemy's offensive and prepare our

counter-offensive. Moreover, quantitatively speaking, we have had to sustain certain losses. Although all the factors favourable to us are having a positive effect, it will not be sufficient to halt the enemy's offensive and to prepare for our counter-offensive unless we make an immense effort. Neither the abolition of corruption and the acceleration of progress at home, nor the curbing of the pro-Japanese forces and the expansion of the anti-Japanese forces abroad, are yet accomplished facts. From all this it follows that our war cannot be won quickly but can only be a protracted war.

## THE THREE STAGES OF THE
## PROTRACTED WAR

35. Since the Sino-Japanese war is a protracted one and final victory will belong to China, it can reasonably be assumed that this protracted war will pass through three stages. The first stage covers the period of the enemy's strategic offensive and our strategic defensive. The second stage will be the period of the enemy's strategic consolidation and our preparation for the counter-offensive. The third stage will be the period of our strategic counter-offensive and the enemy's strategic retreat. It is impossible to predict the concrete situation in the three stages, but certain main trends in the war may be pointed out in the light of present conditions. The objective course of events will be exceedingly rich and varied, with many twists and turns, and nobody can cast a horoscope for the Sino-Japanese war; nevertheless it is necessary for the strategic direction of the war to make a rough sketch of its trends. Although our sketch may not be in full accord with the subsequent facts and will be

amended by them, it is still necessary to make it in order to give firm and purposeful strategic direction to the protracted war.

36. The first stage has not yet ended. The enemy's design is to occupy Canton, Wuhan and Lanchow and link up these three points. To accomplish this aim the enemy will have to use at least fifty divisions, or about one and a half million men, spend from one and a half to two years, and expend more than ten thousand million yen. In penetrating so deeply, he will encounter immense difficulties, with consequences disastrous beyond imagination. As for attempting to occupy the entire length of the Canton-Hankow Railway and the Sian-Lanchow Highway, he will have to fight perilous battles and even so may not fully accomplish his design. But in drawing up our operational plan we should base ourselves on the assumption that the enemy may occupy the three points and even certain additional areas, as well as link them up, and we should make dispositions for a protracted war, so that even if he does so, we shall be able to cope with him. In this stage the form of fighting we should adopt is primarily mobile warfare, supplemented by guerrilla and positional warfare. Through the subjective errors of the Kuomintang military authorities, positional warfare was assigned the primary role in the first phase of this stage, but it is nevertheless supplementary from the point of view of the stage as a whole. In this stage, China has already built up a broad united front and achieved unprecedented unity. Although the enemy has used and will continue to use base and shameless means to induce China to capitulate in the attempt to realize his plan for a quick decision and to conquer the whole country without much effort, he has failed so far, nor is he likely to succeed in the future. In this stage,

in spite of considerable losses, China will make considerable progress, which will become the main basis for her continued resistance in the second stage. In the present stage the Soviet Union has already given substantial aid to China. On the enemy side, there are already signs of flagging morale, and his army's momentum of attack is less in the middle phase of this stage than it was in the initial phase, and it will diminish still further in the concluding phase. Signs of exhaustion are beginning to appear in his finances and economy; war-weariness is beginning to set in among his people and troops; and within the clique at the helm of the war, "war frustrations" are beginning to manifest themselves and pessimism about the prospects of the war is growing.

37. The second stage may be termed one of strategic stalemate. At the tail end of the first stage, the enemy will be forced to fix certain terminal points to his strategic offensive owing to his shortage of troops and our firm resistance, and upon reaching them he will stop his strategic offensive and enter the stage of safeguarding his occupied areas. In the second stage, the enemy will attempt to safeguard the occupied areas and to make them his own by the fraudulent method of setting up puppet governments, while plundering the Chinese people to the limit; but again he will be confronted with stubborn guerrilla warfare. Taking advantage of the fact that the enemy's rear is unguarded, our guerrilla warfare will develop extensively in the first stage, and many base areas will be established, seriously threatening the enemy's consolidation of the occupied areas, and so in the second stage there will still be widespread fighting. In this stage, our form of fighting will be primarily guerrilla warfare, supplemented by mobile warfare. China will still retain a large regular army, but she will find it difficult to launch

the strategic counter-offensive immediately because, on the one hand, the enemy will adopt a strategically defensive position in the big cities and along the main lines of communication under his occupation and, on the other hand, China will not yet be adequately equipped technically. Except for the troops engaged in frontal defence against the enemy, our forces will be switched in large numbers to the enemy's rear in comparatively dispersed dispositions, and, basing themselves on all the areas not actually occupied by the enemy and co-ordinating with the people's local armed forces, they will launch extensive, fierce guerrilla warfare against enemy-occupied areas, keeping the enemy on the move as far as possible in order to destroy him in mobile warfare, as is now being done in Shansi Province. The fighting in the second stage will be ruthless, and the country will suffer serious devastation. But the guerrilla warfare will be successful, and if it is well conducted the enemy may be able to retain only about one-third of his occupied territory, with the remaining two-thirds in our hands, and this will constitute a great defeat for the enemy and a great victory for China. By then the enemy-occupied territory as a whole will fall into three categories: first, the enemy base areas; second, our base areas for guerrilla warfare; and, third, the guerrilla areas contested by both sides. The duration of this stage will depend on the degree of change in the balance of forces between us and the enemy and on the changes in the international situation; generally speaking, we should be prepared to see this stage last a comparatively long time and to weather its hardships. It will be a very painful period for China; the two big problems will be economic difficulties and the disruptive activities of the traitors. The enemy will go all out to wreck China's united front, and the traitor organizations in all the occupied areas will merge into a so-called "unified government". Owing to the loss of big cities and the hardships of war, vacillating elements within our ranks will clamour for compromise, and pessimism will grow to a serious extent. Our tasks will then be to mobilize the whole people to unite as one man and carry on the war with unflinching perseverance, to broaden and consolidate the united front, sweep away all pessimism and ideas of compromise, promote the will to hard struggle and apply new wartime policies, and so to weather the hardships. In the second stage, we will have to call upon the whole country resolutely to maintain a united government, we will have to oppose splits and systematically improve fighting techniques, reform the armed forces, mobilize the entire people and prepare for the counter-offensive. The international situation will become still more unfavourable to Japan and the main international forces will incline towards giving more help to China, even though there may be talk of "realism" of the Chamberlain type which accommodates itself to *faits accomplis*. Japan's threat to Southeast Asia and Siberia will become greater, and there may even be another war. As regards Japan, scores of her divisions will be inextricably bogged down in China. Widespread guerrilla warfare and the people's anti-Japanese movement will wear down this big Japanese force, greatly reducing it and also disintegrating its morale by stimulating the growth of homesickness, war-weariness and even anti-war sentiment. Though it would be wrong to say that Japan will achieve no results at all in her plunder of China, yet, being short of capital and harassed by guerrilla warfare, she cannot possibly achieve rapid or substantial results. This second stage will be the transitional stage of the entire war; it will be the most trying period but also the pivotal one. Whether China becomes an independent country or is reduced to a colony will be determined not by the retention or loss of the big cities in the first stage but by the extent to which the whole nation exerts itself in the second. If we can persevere in the War of Resistance, in the united front and in the protracted war, China will in that stage gain the power to change from weakness to strength. It will be the second act in the three-act drama of China's War of Resistance. And through the efforts of the entire cast it will become possible to perform a most brilliant last act.

38. The third stage will be the stage of the counter-offensive to recover our lost territories. Their recovery will depend mainly upon the strength which China has built up in the preceding stage and which will continue to grow in the third stage. But China's strength alone will not be sufficient, and we shall also have to rely on the support of international forces and on the changes that will take place inside Japan, or otherwise we shall not be able to win; this adds to China's tasks in international propaganda and diplomacy. In the third stage, our war will no longer be one of strategic defensive, but will turn into a strategic counter-offensive manifesting itself in strategic offensives; and it will no longer be fought on strategically interior lines, but will shift gradually to strategically exterior lines. Not until we fight our way to the Yalu River can this war be considered over. The third stage will be the last in the protracted war, and when we talk of persevering in the war to the end, we mean going all the way through this stage. Our primary form of fighting will still be mobile warfare, but positional warfare will rise to importance. While positional defence cannot be regarded as important in the first stage because of the prevailing

circumstances, positional attack will become quite important in the third stage because of the changed conditions and the requirements of the task. In the third stage guerrilla warfare will again provide strategic support by supplementing mobile and positional warfare, but it will not be the primary form as in the second stage.

39. It is thus obvious that the war is protracted and consequently ruthless in nature. The enemy will not be able to gobble up the whole of China but will be able to occupy many places for a considerable time. China will not be able to oust the Japanese quickly, but the greater part of her territory will remain in her hands. Ultimately the enemy will lose and we will win, but we shall have a hard stretch of road to travel.

40. The Chinese people will become tempered in the course of this long and ruthless war. The political parties taking part in the war will also be steeled and tested. The united front must be persevered in; only by persevering in the united front can we persevere in the war; and only by persevering in the united front and in the war can we win final victory. Only thus can all difficulties be overcome. After travelling the hard stretch of road we shall reach the highway to victory. This is the natural logic of the war.

41. In the three stages the changes in relative strength will proceed along the following lines. In the first stage, the enemy is superior and we are inferior in strength. With regard to our inferiority we must reckon on changes of two different kinds from the eve of the War of Resistance to the end of this stage. The first kind is a change for the worse. China's original inferiority will be aggravated by war losses, namely, decreases in territory, population, economic strength, military strength and cultural institutions. Towards the

end of the first stage, the decrease will probably be considerable, especially on the economic side. This point will be exploited by some people as a basis for their theories of national subjugation and of compromise. But the second kind of change, the change for the better, must also be noted. It includes the experience gained in the war, the progress made by the armed forces, the political progress, the mobilization of the people, the development of culture in a new direction, the emergence of guerrilla warfare, the increase in international support, etc. What is on the downgrade in the first stage is the old quantity and the old quality, the manifestations being mainly quantitative. What is on the upgrade is the new quantity and the new quality, the manifestations being mainly qualitative. It is the second kind of change that provides a basis for our ability to fight a protracted war and win final victory.

42. In the first stage, changes of two kinds are also occurring on the enemy's side. The first kind is a change for the worse and manifests itself in hundreds of thousands of casualties, the drain on arms and ammunition, deterioration of troop morale, popular discontent at home, shrinkage of trade, the expenditure of over ten thousand million yen, condemnation by world opinion, etc. This trend also provides a basis for our ability to fight a protracted war and win final victory. But we must likewise reckon with the second kind of change on the enemy's side, a change for the better, that is, his expansion in territory, population and resources. This too is a basis for the protracted nature of our War of Resistance and the impossibility of quick victory, but at the same time certain people will use it as a basis for their theories of national subjugation and of compromise. However, we must take into account the transitory and partial character of this

change for the better on the enemy's side. Japan is an imperialist power heading for collapse, and her occupation of China's territory is temporary. The vigorous growth of guerrilla warfare in China will restrict her actual occupation to narrow zones. Moreover, her occupation of Chinese territory has created and intensified contradictions between Japan and other foreign countries. Besides, generally speaking, such occupation involves a considerable period in which Japan will make capital outlays without drawing any profits, as is shown by the experience in the three northeastern provinces. All of which again gives us a basis for demolishing the theories of national subjugation and of compromise and for establishing the theories of protracted war and of final victory.

43. In the second stage, the above changes on both sides will continue to develop. While the situation cannot be predicted in detail, on the whole Japan will continue on the downgrade and China on the upgrade.[14]   For example, Japan's military and financial resources will be seriously drained by China's guerrilla warfare, popular discontent will grow in Japan, the morale of her troops will deteriorate further, and she will become more isolated internationally. As for China, she will make further progress in the political, military and cultural spheres and in the mobilization of the people; guerrilla warfare will develop further; there will be some new economic growth on the basis of the small industries and the widespread agriculture in the interior; international support will gradually increase; and the whole picture will be quite different from what it is now. This second stage may last quite a long time, during which there will be a great reversal in the balance of forces, with China gradually rising and Japan gradually declining. China will emerge from her inferior position, and Japan will lose her superior

position; first the two countries will become evenly matched, and then their relative positions will be reversed. Thereupon, China will in general have completed her preparations for the strategic counter-offensive and will enter the stage of the counter-offensive and the expulsion of the enemy. It should be reiterated that the change from inferiority to superiority and the completion of preparations for the counter-offensive will involve three things, namely, an increase in China's own strength, an increase in Japan's difficulties, and an increase in international support; it is the combination of all these forces that will bring about China's superiority and the completion of her preparations for the counter-offensive.

44. Because of the unevenness in China's political and economic development, the strategic counter-offensive of the third stage will not present a uniform and even picture throughout the country in its initial phase but will be regional in character, rising here and subsiding there. During this stage, the enemy will not relax his divisive tricks to break China's united front, hence the task of maintaining internal unity in China will become still more important, and we shall have to ensure that the strategic counter-offensive does not collapse halfway through internal dissension. In this period the international situation will become very favourable to China. China's task will be to take advantage of it in order to attain complete liberation and establish an independent democratic state, which at the same time will mean helping the world anti-fascist movement.

45. China moving from inferiority to parity and then to superiority, Japan moving from superiority to parity and then to inferiority; China moving from the defensive to stalemate and then to the counter-offensive, Japan moving from the

offensive to the safeguarding of her gains and then to retreat — such will be the course of the Sino-Japanese war and its inevitable trend.

46. Hence the questions and the conclusions are as follows: Will China be subjugated? The answer is, No, she will not be subjugated, but will win final victory. Can China win quickly? The answer is, No, she cannot win quickly, and the war must be a protracted one. Are these conclusions correct? I think they are.

47. At this point, the exponents of national subjugation and of compromise will again rush in and say, "To move from inferiority to parity China needs a military and economic power equal to Japan's, and to move from parity to superiority she will need a military and economic power greater than Japan's. But this is impossible, hence the above conclusions are not correct."

48. This is the so-called theory that "weapons decide everything",[15] which constitutes a mechanical approach to the question of war and a subjective and one-sided view. Our view is opposed to this; we see not only weapons but also people. Weapons are an important factor in war, but not the decisive factor; it is people, not things, that are decisive. The contest of strength is not only a contest of military and economic power, but also a contest of human power and morale. Military and economic power is necessarily wielded by people. If the great majority of the Chinese, of the Japanese and of the people of other countries are on the side of our War of Resistance Against Japan, how can Japan's military and economic power, wielded as it is by a small minority through coercion, count as superiority? And if not, then does not China, though wielding relatively in-

44

ferior military and economic power, become the superior? There is no doubt that China will gradually grow in military and economic power, provided she perseveres in the War of Resistance and in the united front. As for our enemy, weakened as he will be by the long war and by internal and external contradictions, his military and economic power is bound to change in the reverse direction. In these circumstances, is there any reason why China cannot become the superior? And that is not all. Although we cannot as yet count the military and economic power of other countries as being openly and to any great extent on our side, is there any reason why we will not be able to do so in the future? If Japan's enemy is not just China, if in future one or more other countries make open use of their considerable military and economic power defensively or offensively against Japan and openly help us, then will not our superiority be still greater? Japan is a small country, her war is reactionary and barbarous, and she will become more and more isolated internationally; China is a large country, her war is progressive and just, and she will enjoy more and more support internationally. Is there any reason why the long-term development of these factors should not definitely change the relative position between the enemy and ourselves?

49. The exponents of quick victory, however, do not realize that war is a contest of strength, and that before a certain change has taken place in the relative strength of the belligerents, there is no basis for trying to fight strategically decisive battles and shorten the road to liberation. Were their ideas to be put into practice, we should inevitably run our heads into a brick wall. Or perhaps they are just talking for their own pleasure without really intending to put their ideas into

practice. In the end Mr. Reality will come and pour a bucket of cold water over these chatterers, showing them up as mere windbags who want to get things on the cheap, to have gains without pains. We have had this kind of idle chatter before and we have it now, though not very much so far; but there may be more as the war develops into the stage of stalemate and then of counter-offensive. But in the meantime, if China's losses in the first stage are fairly heavy and the second stage drags on very long, the theories of national subjugation and of compromise will gain great currency. Therefore, our fire should be directed mainly against them and only secondarily against the idle chatter about quick victory.

50. That the war will be protracted is certain, but nobody can predict exactly how many months or years it will last, as this depends entirely upon the degree of the change in the balance of forces. All those who wish to shorten the war have no alternative but to work hard to increase our own strength and reduce that of the enemy. Specifically, the only way is to strive to win more battles and wear down the enemy's forces, develop guerrilla warfare to reduce enemy-occupied territory to a minimum, consolidate and expand the united front to rally the forces of the whole nation, build up new armies and develop new war industries, promote political, economic and cultural progress, mobilize the workers, peasants, businessmen, intellectuals and other sections of the people, disintegrate the enemy forces and win over their soldiers, carry on international propaganda to secure foreign support, and win the support of the Japanese people and other oppressed peoples. Only by doing all this can we reduce the duration of the war. There is no magic short-cut.

# A WAR OF JIG-SAW PATTERN

51. We can say with certainty that the protracted War of Resistance Against Japan will write a splendid page unique in the war history of mankind. One of the special features of this war is the interlocking "jig-saw" pattern which arises from such contradictory factors as the barbarity of Japan and her shortage of troops on the one hand, and the progressiveness of China and the extensiveness of her territory on the other. There have been other wars of jig-saw pattern in history, the three years' civil war in Russia after the October Revolution being a case in point. But what distinguishes this war in China is its especially protracted and extensive character, which will set a record in history. Its jig-saw pattern manifests itself as follows.

52. *Interior and exterior lines.* The anti-Japanese war as a whole is being fought on interior lines; but as far as the relation between the main forces and the guerrilla units is concerned, the former are on the interior lines while the latter are on the exterior lines, presenting a remarkable spectacle of pincers around the enemy. The same can be said of the relationship between the various guerrilla areas. From its own viewpoint each guerrilla area is on interior lines and the other areas are on exterior lines; together they form many battle fronts, which hold the enemy in pincers. In the first stage of the war, the regular army operating strategically on interior lines is withdrawing, but the guerrilla units operating strategically on exterior lines will advance with great strides over wide areas to the rear of the enemy — they will advance even more fiercely in the second stage — thereby presenting a remarkable picture of both withdrawal and advance.

53. *Possession and non-possession of a rear area.* The main forces, which extend the front lines to the outer limits of the enemy's occupied areas, are operating from the rear area of the country as a whole. The guerrilla units, which extend the battle lines into the enemy rear, are separated from the rear area of the country as a whole. But each guerrilla area has a small rear of its own, upon which it relies to establish its fluid battle lines. The case is different with the guerrilla detachments which are dispatched by a guerrilla area for short-term operations in the rear of the enemy in the same area; such detachments have no rear, nor do they have a battle line. "Operating without a rear area" is a special feature of revolutionary war in the new era, wherever a vast territory, a progressive people, and an advanced political party and army are to be found; there is nothing to fear but much to gain from it, and far from having doubts about it we should promote it.

54. *Encirclement and counter-encirclement.* Taking the war as a whole, there is no doubt that we are strategically encircled by the enemy because he is on the strategic offensive and operating on exterior lines while we are on the strategic defensive and operating on interior lines. This is the first form of enemy encirclement. We on our part can encircle one or more of the enemy columns advancing on us along separate routes, because we apply the policy of fighting campaigns and battles from tactically exterior lines by using numerically preponderant forces against these enemy columns advancing on us from strategically exterior lines. This is the first form of our counter-encirclement of the enemy. Next, if we consider the guerrilla base areas in the enemy's rear, each area taken singly is surrounded by the enemy on all sides, like the Wutai Mountains, or on three sides, like the

northwestern Shansi area. This is the second form of enemy encirclement. However, if one considers all the guerrilla base areas together and in their relation to the positions of the regular forces, one can see that we in turn surround a great many enemy forces. In Shansi Province, for instance, we have surrounded the Tatung-Puchow Railway on three sides (the east and west flanks and the southern end) and the city of Taiyuan on all sides; and there are many similar instances in Hopei and Shantung Provinces. This is the second form of our counter-encirclement of the enemy. Thus there are two forms of encirclement by the enemy forces and two forms of encirclement by our own — rather like a game of *weichi*.[16] Campaigns and battles fought by the two sides resemble the capturing of each other's pieces, and the establishment of enemy strongholds (such as Taiyuan) and our guerrilla base areas (such as the Wutai Mountains) resembles moves to dominate spaces on the board. If the game of *weichi* is extended to include the world, there is yet a third form of encirclement as between us and the enemy, namely, the interrelation between the front of aggression and the front of peace. The enemy encircles China, the Soviet Union, France and Czechoslovakia with his front of aggression, while we counter-encircle Germany, Japan and Italy with our front of peace. But our encirclement, like the hand of Buddha, will turn into the Mountain of Five Elements lying athwart the Universe, and the modern Sun Wu-kungs[17] — the fascist aggressors — will finally be buried underneath it, never to rise again. Therefore, if on the international plane we can create an anti-Japanese front in the Pacific region, with China as one strategic unit, with the Soviet Union and other countries which may join it as other strategic units, and with the Japanese people's movement as still

49

another strategic unit, and thus form a gigantic net from which the fascist Sun Wu-kungs can find no escape, then that will be our enemy's day of doom. Indeed, the day when this gigantic net is formed will undoubtedly be the day of the complete overthrow of Japanese imperialism. We are not jesting; this is the inevitable trend of the war.

55. *Big areas and little areas.* There is a possibility that the enemy will occupy the greater part of Chinese territory south of the Great Wall, and only the smaller part will be kept intact. That is one aspect of the situation. But within this greater part, which does not include the three north-eastern provinces, the enemy can actually hold only the big cities, the main lines of communication and some of the plains — which may rank first in importance, but will probably constitute only the smaller part of the occupied territory in size and population, while the greater part will be taken up by the guerrilla areas that will grow up everywhere. That is another aspect of the situation. If we go beyond the provinces south of the Great Wall and include Mongolia, Sinkiang, Chinghai and Tibet, then the unoccupied area will constitute the greater part of China's territory, and the enemy-occupied area will become the smaller part, even with the three northeastern provinces. That is yet another aspect of the situation. The area kept intact is undoubtedly important, and we should devote great efforts to developing it, not only politically, militarily and economically but, what is also important, culturally. The enemy has transformed our former cultural centres into culturally backward areas, and we on our part must transform the former culturally backward areas into cultural centres. At the same time, the work of developing extensive guerrilla areas behind the enemy lines is also extremely important, and we should attend to every

aspect of this work, including the cultural. All in all, big pieces of China's territory, namely, the rural areas, will be transformed into regions of progress and light, while the small pieces, namely, the enemy-occupied areas and especially the big cities, will temporarily become regions of backwardness and darkness.

56. Thus it can be seen that the protracted and far-flung War of Resistance Against Japan is a war of a jig-saw pattern militarily, politically, economically and culturally. It is a marvellous spectacle in the annals of war, a heroic undertaking by the Chinese nation, a magnificent and earth-shaking feat. This war will not only affect China and Japan, strongly impelling both to advance, but will also affect the whole world, impelling all nations, especially the oppressed nations such as India, to march forward. Every Chinese should consciously throw himself into this war of a jig-saw pattern, for this is the form of war by which the Chinese nation is liberating itself, the special form of war of liberation waged by a big semi-colonial country in the Nineteen Thirties and the Nineteen Forties.


## FIGHTING FOR PERPETUAL PEACE

57. The protracted nature of China's anti-Japanese war is inseparably connected with the fight for perpetual peace in China and the whole world. Never has there been a historical period such as the present in which war is so close to perpetual peace. For several thousand years since the emergence of classes, the life of mankind has been full of wars; each nation has fought countless wars, either internally or with other nations. In the imperialist epoch of capitalist

society, wars are waged on a particularly extensive scale and with a peculiar ruthlessness. The first great imperialist war of twenty years ago was the first of its kind in history, but not the last. Only the war which has now begun comes close to being the final war, that is, comes close to the perpetual peace of mankind. By now one-third of the world's population has entered the war. Look! Italy, then Japan; Abyssinia, then Spain, then China. The population of the countries at war now amounts to almost 600 million, or nearly a third of the total population of the world. The characteristics of the present war are its uninterruptedness and its proximity to perpetual peace. Why is it uninterrupted? After attacking Abyssinia, Italy attacked Spain, and Germany joined in; then Japan attacked China. What will come next? Undoubtedly Hitler will fight the great powers. "Fascism is war"[18] — this is perfectly true. There will be no interruption in the development of the present war into a world war; mankind will not be able to avoid the calamity of war. Why then do we say the present war is near to perpetual peace? The present war is the result of the development of the general crisis of world capitalism which began with World War I; this general crisis is driving the capitalist countries into a new war and, above all, driving the fascist countries into new war adventures. This war, we can foresee, will not save capitalism, but will hasten its collapse. It will be greater in scale and more ruthless than the war of twenty years ago, all nations will inevitably be drawn in, it will drag on for a very long time, and mankind will suffer greatly. But, owing to the existence of the Soviet Union and the growing political consciousness of the people of the world, great revolutionary wars will undoubtedly emerge from this war to oppose all counter-revolutionary wars, thus giving this war the character of a struggle for perpetual peace. Even if later there should be another period of war, perpetual world peace will not be far off. Once man has eliminated capitalism, he will attain the era of perpetual peace, and there will be no more need for war. Neither armies, nor warships, nor military aircraft, nor poison gas will then be needed. Thereafter and for all time, mankind will never again know war. The revolutionary wars which have already begun are part of the war for perpetual peace. The war between China and Japan, two countries which have a combined population of over 500 million, will take an important place in this war for perpetual peace, and out of it will come the liberation of the Chinese nation. The liberated new China of the future will be inseparable from the liberated new world of the future. Hence our War of Resistance Against Japan takes on the character of a struggle for perpetual peace.

58. History shows that wars are divided into two kinds, just and unjust. All wars that are progressive are just, and all wars that impede progress are unjust. We Communists oppose all unjust wars that impede progress, but we do not oppose progressive, just wars. Not only do we Communists not oppose just wars, we actively participate in them. As for unjust wars, World War I is an instance in which both sides fought for imperialist interests; therefore the Communists of the whole world firmly opposed that war. The way to oppose a war of this kind is to do everything possible to prevent it before it breaks out and, once it breaks out, to oppose war with war, to oppose unjust war with just war, whenever possible. Japan's war is an unjust war that impedes progress, and the peoples of the world, including the Japanese people, should oppose it and are opposing it. In our country

the people and the government, the Communist Party and the Kuomintang, have all raised the banner of righteousness in the national revolutionary war against aggression. Our war is sacred and just, it is progressive and its aim is peace. The aim is peace not just in one country but throughout the world, not just temporary but perpetual peace. To achieve this aim we must wage a life-and-death struggle, be prepared for any sacrifice, persevere to the end and never stop short of the goal. However great the sacrifice and however long the time needed to attain it, a new world of perpetual peace and brightness already lies clearly before us. Our faith in waging this war is based upon the new China and the new world of perpetual peace and brightness for which we are striving. Fascism and imperialism wish to perpetuate war, but we wish to put an end to it in the not too distant future. The great majority of mankind should exert their utmost efforts for this purpose. The 450 million people of China constitute one quarter of the world's population, and if by their concerted efforts they overthrow Japanese imperialism and create a new China of freedom and equality, they will most certainly be making a tremendous contribution to the struggle for perpetual world peace. This is no vain hope, for the whole world is approaching this point in the course of its social and economic development, and provided that the majority of mankind work together, our goal will surely be attained in several decades.

## MAN'S DYNAMIC ROLE IN WAR

59. We have so far explained why the war is a protracted war and why the final victory will be China's, and in the

main dealt with what protracted war is and what it is not. Now we shall turn to the question of what to do and what not to do. How to conduct protracted war and how to win the final victory? These are the questions answered below. We shall therefore successively discuss the following problems: man's dynamic role in war, war and politics, political mobilization for the War of Resistance, the object of war, offence within defence, quick decisions within a protracted war, exterior lines within interior lines, initiative, flexibility, planning, mobile warfare, guerrilla warfare, positional warfare, war of annihilation, war of attrition, the possibilities of exploiting the enemy's mistakes, the question of decisive engagements in the anti-Japanese war, and the army and the people as the foundation of victory. Let us start with the problem of man's dynamic role.

60. When we say we are opposed to a subjective approach to problems, we mean that we must oppose ideas which are not based upon or do not correspond to objective facts, because such ideas are fanciful and fallacious and will lead to failure if acted on. But whatever is done has to be done by human beings; protracted war and final victory will not come about without human action. For such action to be effective there must be people who derive ideas, principles or views from the objective facts, and put forward plans, directives, policies, strategies and tactics. Ideas, etc. are subjective, while deeds or actions are the subjective translated into the objective, but both represent the dynamic role peculiar to human beings. We term this kind of dynamic role "man's conscious dynamic role", and it is a characteristic that distinguishes man from all other beings. All ideas based upon and corresponding to objective facts are correct ideas, and all deeds or actions based upon correct ideas are

correct actions. We must give full scope to these ideas and actions, to this dynamic role. The anti-Japanese war is being waged to drive out imperialism and transform the old China into a new China; this can be achieved only when the whole Chinese people are mobilized and full scope is given to their conscious dynamic role in resisting Japan. If we just sit by and take no action, only subjugation awaits us and there will be neither protracted war nor final victory.

61. It is a human characteristic to exercise a conscious dynamic role. Man strongly displays this characteristic in war. True, victory or defeat in war is decided by the military, political, economic and geographical conditions on both sides, the nature of the war each side is waging and the international support each enjoys, but it is not decided by these alone; in themselves, all these provide only the possibility of victory or defeat but do not decide the issue. To decide the issue, subjective effort must be added, namely, the directing and waging of war, man's conscious dynamic role in war.

62. In seeking victory, those who direct a war cannot overstep the limitations imposed by the objective conditions; within these limitations, however, they can and must play a dynamic role in striving for victory. The stage of action for commanders in a war must be built upon objective possibilities, but on that stage they can direct the performance of many a drama, full of sound and colour, power and grandeur. Given the objective material foundations, the commanders in the anti-Japanese war should display their prowess and marshal all their forces to crush the national enemy, transform the present situation in which our country and society are suffering from aggression and oppression, and create a new China of freedom and equality; here is where our subjective faculties for directing war can and must be exercised.

We do not want any of our commanders in the war to detach himself from the objective conditions and become a blundering hothead, but we decidedly want every commander to become a general who is both bold and sagacious. Our commanders should have not only the boldness to overwhelm the enemy but also the ability to remain masters of the situation throughout the changes and vicissitudes of the entire war. Swimming in the ocean of war, they must not flounder but make sure of reaching the opposite shore with measured strokes. Strategy and tactics, as the laws for directing war, constitute the art of swimming in the ocean of war.

## WAR AND POLITICS

63. "War is the continuation of politics." In this sense war is politics and war itself is a political action; since ancient times there has never been a war that did not have a political character. The anti-Japanese war is a revolutionary war waged by the whole nation, and victory is inseparable from the political aim of the war — to drive out Japanese imperialism and build a new China of freedom and equality — inseparable from the general policy of persevering in the War of Resistance and in the united front, from the mobilization of the entire people, and from the political principles of the unity between officers and men, the unity between army and people and the disintegration of the enemy forces, and inseparable from the effective application of united front policy, from mobilization on the cultural front, and from the efforts to win international support and the support of the people inside Japan. In a word, war cannot for a single moment be separated from politics. Any

tendency among the anti-Japanese armed forces to belittle politics by isolating war from it and advocating the idea of war as an absolute is wrong and should be corrected.

64. But war has its own particular characteristics and in this sense it cannot be equated with politics in general. "War is the continuation of politics by other . . . means."[19] When politics develops to a certain stage beyond which it cannot proceed by the usual means, war breaks out to sweep the obstacles from the way. For instance, the semi-independent status of China is an obstacle to the political growth of Japanese imperialism, hence Japan has unleashed a war of aggression to sweep away that obstacle. What about China? Imperialist oppression has long been an obstacle to China's bourgeois-democratic revolution, hence many wars of liberation have been waged in the effort to sweep it away. Japan is now using war for the purpose of oppressing China and completely blocking the advance of the Chinese revolution, and therefore China is compelled to wage the War of Resistance in her determination to sweep away this obstacle. When the obstacle is removed, our political aim will be attained and the war concluded. But if the obstacle is not completely swept away, the war will have to continue till the aim is fully accomplished. Thus anyone who seeks a compromise before the task of the anti-Japanese war is fulfilled is bound to fail, because even if a compromise were to occur for one reason or another, the war would break out again, since the broad masses of the people would certainly not submit but would continue the war until its political objective was achieved. It can therefore be said that politics is war without bloodshed while war is politics with bloodshed.

65. From the particular characteristics of war there arise a particular set of organizations, a particular series of methods and a particular kind of process. The organizations are the armed forces and everything that goes with them. The methods are the strategy and tactics for directing war. The process is the particular form of social activity in which the opposing armed forces attack each other or defend themselves against one another, employing strategy and tactics favourable to themselves and unfavourable to the enemy. Hence war experience is a particular kind of experience. All who take part in war must rid themselves of their customary ways and accustom themselves to war before they can win victory.

## POLITICAL MOBILIZATION FOR THE WAR OF RESISTANCE

66. A national revolutionary war as great as ours cannot be won without extensive and thoroughgoing political mobilization. Before the anti-Japanese war there was no political mobilization for resistance to Japan, and this was a great drawback, as a result of which China has already lost a move to the enemy. After the war began, political mobilization was very far from extensive, let alone thoroughgoing. It was the enemy's gunfire and the bombs dropped by enemy aeroplanes that brought news of the war to the great majority of the people. That was also a kind of mobilization, but it was done for us by the enemy, we did not do it ourselves. Even now the people in the remoter regions beyond the noise of the guns are carrying on quietly as usual. This situation must change, or otherwise we cannot win in our life-and-

death struggle. We must never lose another move to the enemy; on the contrary, we must make full use of this move, political mobilization, to get the better of him. This move is crucial; it is indeed of primary importance, while our inferiority in weapons and other things is only secondary. The mobilization of the common people throughout the country will create a vast sea in which to drown the enemy, create the conditions that will make up for our inferiority in arms and other things, and create the prerequisites for overcoming every difficulty in the war. To win victory, we must persevere in the War of Resistance, in the united front and in the protracted war. But all these are inseparable from the mobilization of the common people. To wish for victory and yet neglect political mobilization is like wishing to "go south by driving the chariot north", and the result would inevitably be to forfeit victory.

67. What does political mobilization mean? First, it means telling the army and the people about the political aim of the war. It is necessary for every soldier and civilian to see why the war must be fought and how it concerns him. The political aim of the war is "to drive out Japanese imperialism and build a new China of freedom and equality"; we must proclaim this aim to everybody, to all soldiers and civilians, before we can create an anti-Japanese upsurge and unite hundreds of millions as one man to contribute their all to the war. Secondly, it is not enough merely to explain the aim to them; the steps and policies for its attainment must also be given, that is, there must be a political programme. We already have the Ten-Point Programme for Resisting Japan and Saving the Nation and also the Programme of Armed Resistance and National Reconstruction; we should popularize both of them in the army and

among the people and mobilize everyone to carry them out. Without a clear-cut, concrete political programme it is impossible to mobilize all the armed forces and the whole people to carry the war against Japan through to the end. Thirdly, how should we mobilize them? By word of mouth, by leaflets and bulletins, by newspapers, books and pamphlets, through plays and films, through schools, through the mass organizations and through our cadres. What has been done so far in the Kuomintang areas is only a drop in the ocean, and moreover it has been done in a manner ill-suited to the people's tastes and in a spirit uncongenial to them; this must be drastically changed. Fourthly, to mobilize once is not enough; political mobilization for the War of Resistance must be continuous. Our job is not to recite our political programme to the people, for nobody will listen to such recitations; we must link the political mobilization for the war with developments in the war and with the life of the soldiers and the people, and make it a continuous movement. This is a matter of immense importance on which our victory in the war primarily depends.

## THE OBJECT OF WAR

68. Here we are not dealing with the political aim of war; the political aim of the War of Resistance Against Japan has been defined above as "to drive out Japanese imperialism and build a new China of freedom and equality". Here we are dealing with the elementary object of war, war as "politics with bloodshed", as mutual slaughter by opposing armies. The object of war is specifically "to preserve oneself and destroy the enemy" (to destroy the enemy means to disarm him or "deprive him of the power to resist", and does

not mean to destroy every member of his forces physically). In ancient warfare, the spear and the shield were used, the spear to attack and destroy the enemy, and the shield to defend and preserve oneself. To the present day, all weapons are still an extension of the spear and the shield. The bomber, the machine-gun, the long-range gun and poison gas are developments of the spear, while the air-raid shelter, the steel helmet, the concrete fortification and the gas mask are developments of the shield. The tank is a new weapon combining the functions of both spear and shield. Attack is the chief means of destroying the enemy, but defence cannot be dispensed with. In attack the immediate object is to destroy the enemy, but at the same time it is self-preservation, because if the enemy is not destroyed, you will be destroyed. In defence the immediate object is to preserve yourself, but at the same time defence is a means of supplementing attack or preparing to go over to the attack. Retreat is in the category of defence and is a continuation of defence, while pursuit is a continuation of attack. It should be pointed out that destruction of the enemy is the primary object of war and self-preservation the secondary, because only by destroying the enemy in large numbers can one effectively preserve oneself. Therefore attack, the chief means of destroying the enemy, is primary, while defence, a supplementary means of destroying the enemy and a means of self-preservation, is secondary. In actual warfare the chief role is played by defence much of the time and by attack for the rest of the time, but if war is taken as a whole, attack remains primary.

69. How do we justify the encouragement of heroic sacrifice in war? Does it not contradict "self-preservation"? No, it does not; sacrifice and self-preservation are both opposite and complementary to each other. War is politics with

bloodshed and exacts a price, sometimes an extremely high price. Partial and temporary sacrifice (non-preservation) is incurred for the sake of general and permanent preservation. This is precisely why we say that attack, which is basically a means of destroying the enemy, also has the function of self-preservation. It is also the reason why defence must be accompanied by attack and should not be defence pure and simple.

70. The object of war, namely, the preservation of oneself and the destruction of the enemy, is the essence of war and the basis of all war activities, an essence which pervades all war activities, from the technical to the strategic. The object of war is the underlying principle of war, and no technical, tactical, or strategic concepts or principles can in any way depart from it. What for instance is meant by the principle of "taking cover and making full use of fire-power" in shooting? The purpose of the former is self-preservation, of the latter the destruction of the enemy. The former gives rise to such techniques as making use of the terrain and its features, advancing in spurts, and spreading out in dispersed formation. The latter gives rise to other techniques, such as clearing the field of fire and organizing a fire-net. As for the assault force, the containing force and the reserve force in a tactical operation, the first is for annihilating the enemy, the second for preserving oneself, and the third is for either purpose according to circumstances — either for annihilating the enemy (in which case it reinforces the assault force or serves as a pursuit force), or for self-preservation (in which case it reinforces the containing force or serves as a covering force). Thus, no technical, tactical, or strategical principles or operations can in any way depart from the object of war,

and this object pervades the whole of a war and runs through it from beginning to end.

71. In directing the anti-Japanese war, leaders at the various levels must lose sight neither of the contrast between the fundamental factors on each side nor of the object of this war. In the course of military operations these contrasting fundamental factors unfold themselves in the struggle by each side to preserve itself and destroy the other. In our war we strive in every engagement to win a victory, big or small, and to disarm a part of the enemy and destroy a part of his men and *matériel*. We must accumulate the results of these partial destructions of the enemy into major strategic victories and so achieve the final political aim of expelling the enemy, protecting the motherland and building a new China.

## OFFENCE WITHIN DEFENCE,
## QUICK DECISIONS WITHIN A PROTRACTED WAR,
## EXTERIOR LINES WITHIN INTERIOR LINES

72. Now let us examine the specific strategy of the War of Resistance Against Japan. We have already said that our strategy for resisting Japan is that of protracted war, and indeed this is perfectly right. But this strategy is general, not specific. Specifically, how should the protracted war be conducted? We shall now discuss this question. Our answer is as follows. In the first and second stages of the war, *i.e.*, in the stages of the enemy's offensive and preservation of his gains, we should conduct tactical offensives within the strategic defensive, campaigns and battles of quick decision within the strategically protracted war, and campaigns and battles on exterior lines within strategically interior lines.

In the third stage, we should launch the strategic counter-offensive.

73. Since Japan is a strong imperialist power and we are a weak semi-colonial and semi-feudal country, she has adopted the policy of the strategic offensive while we are on the strategic defensive. Japan is trying to execute the strategy of a war of quick decision; we should consciously execute the strategy of protracted war. Japan is using dozens of army divisions of fairly high combat effectiveness (now numbering thirty) and part of her navy to encircle and blockade China from both land and sea, and is using her air force to bomb China. Her army has already established a long front stretching from Paotow to Hangchow and her navy has reached Fukien and Kwangtung; thus exterior-line operations have taken shape on a vast scale. On the other hand, we are in the position of operating on interior lines. All this is due to the fact that the enemy is strong while we are weak. This is one aspect of the situation.

74. But there is another and exactly opposite aspect. Japan, though strong, does not have enough soldiers. China, though weak, has a vast territory, a large population and plenty of soldiers. Two important consequences follow. First, the enemy, employing his small forces against a vast country, can only occupy some big cities and main lines of communication and part of the plains. Thus there are extensive areas in the territory under his occupation which he has had to leave ungarrisoned, and which provide a vast arena for our guerrilla warfare. Taking China as a whole, even if the enemy manages to occupy the line connecting Canton, Wuhan and Lanchow and its adjacent areas, he can hardly seize the regions beyond, and this gives China a general rear and vital bases from which to carry on the protracted war to

final victory. Secondly, in pitting his small forces against large forces, the enemy is encircled by our large forces. The enemy is attacking us along several routes, strategically he is on exterior lines while we are on interior lines, strategically he is on the offensive while we are on the defensive; all this looks very much to our disadvantage. However, we can make use of our two advantages, namely, our vast territory and large forces, and, instead of stubborn positional warfare, carry on flexible mobile warfare, employing several divisions against one enemy division, several tens of thousands of our men against ten thousand of his, several columns against one of his columns, and suddenly encircling and attacking a single column from the exterior lines of the battlefield. In this way, while the enemy is on exterior lines and on the offensive in strategic operations, he will be forced to fight on interior lines and on the defensive in campaigns and battles. And for us, interior lines and the defensive in strategic operations will be transformed into exterior lines and the offensive in campaigns and battles. This is the way to deal with one or indeed with any advancing enemy column. Both the consequences discussed above follow from the fact that the enemy is small while we are big. Moreover, the enemy forces, though small, are strong (in arms and in training) while our forces, though large, are weak (in arms and in training but not in morale), and in campaigns and battles, therefore, we should not only employ large forces against small and operate from exterior against interior lines, but also follow the policy of seeking quick decisions. In general, to achieve quick decision, we should attack a moving and not a stationary enemy. We should concentrate a big force under cover beforehand alongside the route which the enemy is sure to take, and while he is on the move, advance suddenly to encircle and attack him before he knows what is happening, and thus quickly conclude the battle. If we fight well, we may destroy the entire enemy force or the greater part or some part of it, and even if we do not fight so well, we may still inflict heavy casualties. This applies to any and every one of our battles. If each month we could win one sizable victory like that at Pinghsingkuan or Taierhchuang, not to speak of more, it would greatly demoralize the enemy, stimulate the morale of our own forces and evoke international support. Thus our strategically protracted war is translated in the field into battles of quick decision. The enemy's war of strategic quick decision is bound to change into protracted war after he is defeated in many campaigns and battles.

75. In a word, the above operational principle for fighting campaigns and battles is one of "quick-decision offensive warfare on exterior lines". It is the opposite of our strategic principle of "protracted defensive warfare on interior lines", and yet it is the indispensable principle for carrying out this strategy. If we should use "protracted defensive warfare on interior lines" as the principle for campaigns and battles too, as we did at the beginning of the War of Resistance, it would be totally unsuited to the circumstances in which the enemy is small while we are big and the enemy is strong while we are weak; in that case we could never achieve our strategic objective of a protracted war and we would be defeated by the enemy. That is why we have always advocated the organization of the forces of the entire country into a number of large field armies, each counterposed to one of the enemy's field armies but having two, three or four times its strength, and so keeping the enemy engaged in extensive theatres of war in accordance with the principle outlined above. This

principle of "quick-decision offensive warfare on exterior lines" can and must be applied in guerrilla as well as in regular warfare. It is applicable not only to any one stage of the war but to its entire course. In the stage of strategic counter-offensive, when we are better equipped technically and are no longer in the position of the weak fighting the strong, we shall be able to capture prisoners and booty on a large scale all the more effectively if we continue to employ superior numbers in quick-decision offensive battles from exterior lines. For instance, if we employ two, three or four mechanized divisions against one mechanized enemy division, we can be all the more certain of destroying it. It is common sense that several hefty fellows can easily beat one.

76. If we resolutely apply "quick-decision offensive warfare on exterior lines" on a battlefield, we shall not only change the balance of forces on that battlefield, but also gradually change the general situation. On the battlefield we shall be on the offensive and the enemy on the defensive, we shall be employing superior numbers on exterior lines and the enemy inferior numbers on interior lines, and we shall seek quick decisions, while the enemy, try as he may, will not be able to protract the fighting in the expectation of reinforcements; for all these reasons, the enemy's position will change from strong to weak, from superior to inferior, while that of our forces will change from weak to strong, from inferior to superior. After many such battles have been victoriously fought, the general situation between us and the enemy will change. That is to say, through the accumulation of victories on many battlefields by quick-decision offensive warfare on exterior lines, we shall gradually strengthen ourselves and weaken the enemy, which will necessarily affect the general balance of forces and bring about changes in it.

When that happens, these changes, together with other factors on our side and together with the changes inside the enemy camp and a favourable international situation, will turn the over-all situation between us and the enemy first into one of parity and then into one of superiority for us. That will be the time for us to launch the counter-offensive and drive the enemy out of the country.

77. War is a contest of strength, but the original pattern of strength changes in the course of war. Here the decisive factor is subjective effort — winning more victories and committing fewer errors. The objective factors provide the possibility for such change, but in order to turn this possibility into actuality both correct policy and subjective effort are essential. It is then that the subjective plays the decisive role.

## INITIATIVE, FLEXIBILITY AND PLANNING

78. In quick-decision offensive campaigns and battles on exterior lines, as discussed above, the crucial point is the "offensive"; "exterior lines" refers to the sphere of the offensive and "quick-decision" to its duration. Hence the name "quick-decision offensive warfare on exterior lines". It is the best principle for waging a protracted war and it is also the principle for what is known as mobile warfare. But it cannot be put into effect without initiative, flexibility and planning. Let us now study these three questions.

79. We have already discussed man's conscious dynamic role, so why do we talk about the initiative again? By conscious dynamic role we mean conscious action and effort, a characteristic distinguishing man from other beings, and this

human characteristic manifests itself most strongly in war; all this has been discussed already. The initiative here means an army's freedom of action as distinguished from an enforced loss of freedom. Freedom of action is the very life of an army and, once it is lost, the army is close to defeat or destruction. The disarming of a soldier is the result of his losing freedom of action through being forced into a passive position. The same is true of the defeat of an army. For this reason both sides in war do all they can to gain the initiative and avoid passivity. It may be said that the quick-decision offensive warfare on exterior lines which we advocate and the flexibility and planning necessary for its execution are designed to gain the initiative and thus force the enemy into a passive position and achieve the object of preserving ourselves and destroying the enemy. But initiative or passivity is inseparable from superiority or inferiority in the capacity to wage war. Consequently it is also inseparable from the correctness or incorrectness of the subjective direction of war. In addition, there is the question of exploiting the enemy's misconceptions and unpreparedness in order to gain the initiative and force the enemy into passivity. These points are analysed below.

80. Initiative is inseparable from superiority in capacity to wage war, while passivity is inseparable from inferiority in capacity to wage war. Such superiority or inferiority is the objective basis of initiative or passivity. It is natural that the strategic initiative can be better maintained and exercised through a strategic offensive, but to maintain the initiative always and everywhere, that is, to have the absolute initiative, is possible only when there is absolute superiority matched against absolute inferiority. When a strong, healthy man wrestles with an invalid, he has the absolute initiative. If

Japan were not riddled with insoluble contradictions, if, for instance, she could throw in a huge force of several million or ten million men all at once, if her financial resources were several times what they are, if she had no opposition from her own people or from other countries, and if she did not pursue the barbarous policies which arouse the desperate resistance of the Chinese people, then she would be able to maintain absolute superiority and have the absolute initiative always and everywhere. In history, such absolute superiority rarely appears in the early stages of a war or a campaign but is to be found towards its end. For instance, on the eve of Germany's capitulation in World War I, the Entente countries became absolutely superior and Germany absolutely inferior, so that Germany was defeated and the Entente countries were victorious; this is an example of absolute superiority and inferiority towards the end of a war. Again, on the eve of the Chinese victory at Taierhchuang, the isolated Japanese forces there were reduced after bitter fighting to absolute inferiority while our forces achieved absolute superiority, so that the enemy was defeated and we were victorious; this is an example of absolute superiority and inferiority towards the end of a campaign. A war or campaign may also end in a situation of relative superiority or of parity, in which case there is compromise in the war or stalemate in the campaign. But in most cases it is absolute superiority and inferiority that decide victory and defeat. All this holds for the end of a war or a campaign, and not for the beginning. The outcome of the Sino-Japanese war, it can be predicted, will be that Japan will become absolutely inferior and be defeated and that China will become absolutely superior and gain victory. But at present superiority or inferiority is not absolute on either side, but is relative. With the advantages of her military, economic and political-organizational power, Japan enjoys superiority over us with our military, economic and political-organizational weakness, which creates the basis for her initiative. But since quantitatively her military and other power is not great and she has many other disadvantages, her superiority is reduced by her own contradictions. Upon her invasion of China, her superiority has been reduced still further because she has come up against our vast territory, large population, great numbers of troops and resolute nation-wide resistance. Hence, Japan's general position has become one of only relative superiority, and her ability to exercise and maintain the initiative, which is thereby restricted, has likewise become relative. As for China, though placed in a somewhat passive position strategically because of her inferior strength, she is nevertheless quantitatively superior in territory, population and troops, and also superior in the morale of her people and army and their patriotic hatred of the enemy; this superiority, together with other advantages, reduces the extent of her inferiority in military, economic and other power, and changes it into a relative strategic inferiority. This also reduces the degree of China's passivity so that her strategic position is one of only relative passivity. Any passivity, however, is a disadvantage, and one must strive hard to shake it off. Militarily, the way to do so is resolutely to wage quick-decision offensive warfare on exterior lines, to launch guerrilla warfare in the rear of the enemy and so secure overwhelming local superiority and initiative in many campaigns of mobile and guerrilla warfare. Through such local superiority and local initiative in many campaigns, we can gradually create strategic superiority and strategic initiative and extricate ourselves from strategic inferiority and passivity. Such is the interrelation between initiative and passivity, between superiority and inferiority.

81. From this we can also understand the relationship between initiative or passivity and the subjective directing of war. As already explained, it is possible to escape from our position of relative strategic inferiority and passivity, and the method is to create local superiority and initiative in many campaigns, so depriving the enemy of local superiority and initiative and plunging him into inferiority and passivity. These local successes will add up to strategic superiority and initiative for us and strategic inferiority and passivity for the enemy. Such a change depends upon correct subjective direction. Why? Because while we seek superiority and the initiative, so does the enemy; viewed from this angle, war is a contest in subjective ability between the commanders of the opposing armies in their struggle for superiority and for the initiative on the basis of material conditions such as military forces and financial resources. Out of the contest there emerge a victor and a vanquished; leaving aside the contrast in objective material conditions, the victor will necessarily owe his success to correct subjective direction and the vanquished his defeat to wrong subjective direction. We admit that the phenomenon of war is more elusive and is characterized by greater uncertainty than any other social phenomenon, in other words, that it is more a matter of "probability". Yet war is in no way supernatural, but a mundane process governed by necessity. That is why Sun Wu Tzu's axiom, "Know the enemy and know yourself, and you can fight a hundred battles with no danger of defeat",[20] remains a scientific truth. Mistakes arise from ignorance about the enemy and about ourselves, and moreover the peculiar nature of war makes it impossible in many cases to have full

knowledge about both sides; hence the uncertainty about military conditions and operations, and hence mistakes and defeats. But whatever the situation and the moves in a war, one can know their general aspects and essential points. It is possible for a commander to reduce errors and give generally correct direction, first through all kinds of reconnaissance and then through intelligent inference and judgement. Armed with the weapon of "generally correct direction", we can win more battles and transform our inferiority into superiority and our passivity into initiative. This is how initiative or passivity is related to the correct or incorrect subjective direction of a war.

82. The thesis that incorrect subjective direction can change superiority and initiative into inferiority and passivity, and that correct subjective direction can effect a reverse change, becomes all the more convincing when we look at the record of defeats suffered by big and powerful armies and of victories won by small and weak armies. There are many such instances in Chinese and foreign history. Examples in China are the Battle of Chengpu between the states of Tsin and Chu,[21] the Battle of Chengkao between the states of Chu and Han,[22] the Battle in which Han Hsin defeated the Chao armies,[23] the Battle of Kunyang between the states of Hsin and Han,[24] the Battle of Kuantu between Yuan Shao and Tsao Tsao,[25] the Battle of Chihpi between the states of Wu and Wei,[26] the Battle of Yiling between the states of Wu and Shu,[27] the Battle of Feishui between the states of Chin and Tsin,[28] etc. Among examples to be found abroad are most of Napoleon's campaigns and the civil war in the Soviet Union after the October Revolution. In all these instances, victory was won by small forces over big and by inferior over superior forces. In every case, the weaker force, pitting local su-

periority and initiative against the enemy's local inferiority and passivity, first inflicted one sharp defeat on the enemy and then turned on the rest of his forces and smashed them one by one, thus transforming the over-all situation into one of superiority and initiative. The reverse was the case with the enemy who originally had superiority and held the initiative; owing to subjective errors and internal contradictions, it sometimes happened that he completely lost an excellent or fairly good position in which he enjoyed superiority and initiative, and became a general without an army or a king without a kingdom. Thus it can be seen that although superiority or inferiority in the capacity to wage war is the objective basis determining initiative or passivity, it is not in itself actual initiative or passivity; it is only through a struggle, a contest of ability, that actual initiative or passivity can emerge. In the struggle, correct subjective direction can transform inferiority into superiority and passivity into initiative, and incorrect subjective direction can do the opposite. The fact that every ruling dynasty was defeated by revolutionary armies shows that mere superiority in certain respects does not guarantee the initiative, much less the final victory. The inferior side can wrest the initiative and victory from the superior side by securing certain conditions through active subjective endeavour in accordance with the actual circumstances.

83. To have misconceptions and to be caught unawares may mean to lose superiority and initiative. Hence, deliberately creating misconceptions for the enemy and then springing surprise attacks upon him are two ways — indeed two important means — of achieving superiority and seizing the initiative. What are misconceptions? "To see every bush and tree on Mount Pakung as an enemy soldier"[29] is an

example of misconception. And "making a feint to the east but attacking in the west" is a way of creating misconceptions among the enemy. When the mass support is sufficiently good to block the leakage of news, it is often possible by various ruses to succeed in leading the enemy into a morass of wrong judgements and actions so that he loses his superiority and the initiative. The saying, "There can never be too much deception in war", means precisely this. What does "being caught unawares" mean? It means being unprepared. Without preparedness superiority is not real superiority and there can be no initiative either. Having grasped this point, a force which is inferior but prepared can often defeat a superior enemy by surprise attack. We say an enemy on the move is easy to attack precisely because he is then off guard, that is, unprepared. These two points — creating misconceptions among the enemy and springing surprise attacks on him — mean transferring the uncertainties of war to the enemy while securing the greatest possible certainty for ourselves and thereby gaining superiority, the initiative and victory. Excellent organization of the masses is the prerequisite for attaining all this. Therefore it is extremely important to arouse all the people who are opposed to the enemy, to arm themselves to the last man, make widespread raids on the enemy and also prevent the leakage of news and provide a screen for our own forces; in this way the enemy will be kept in the dark about where and when our forces will attack, and an objective basis will be created for misconceptions and unpreparedness on his part. It was largely owing to the organized, armed masses of the people that the weak and small force of the Chinese Red Army was able to win many battles in the period of the Agrarian Revolutionary War. Logically, a national war should win broader mass support than an agrarian revolutionary war; however, as a result of past mistakes[30] the people are in an unorganized state, cannot be promptly drawn in to serve the cause and are sometimes even made use of by the enemy. The resolute rallying of the people on a broad scale is the only way to secure inexhaustible resources to meet all the requirements of the war. Moreover, it will definitely play a big part in carrying out our tactics of defeating the enemy by misleading him and catching him unawares. We are not Duke Hsiang of Sung and have no use for his asinine ethics.[31] In order to achieve victory we must as far as possible make the enemy blind and deaf by sealing his eyes and ears and drive his commanders to distraction by creating confusion in their minds. The above concerns the way in which the initiative or passivity is related to the subjective direction of the war. Such subjective direction is indispensable for defeating Japan.

84. By and large, Japan has held the initiative in the stage of her offensive by reason of her military power and her exploitation of our subjective errors, past and present. But her initiative is beginning to wane to some extent because of her many inherent disadvantages and of the subjective errors she too has committed in the course of the war (of which more later) and also because of our many advantages. The enemy's defeat at Taierhchuang and his predicament in Shansi prove this clearly. The widespread development of guerrilla warfare in the enemy's rear has placed his garrisons in the occupied areas in a completely passive position. Although he is still on the offensive strategically and still holds the initiative, his initiative will end when his strategic offensive ends. The first reason why the enemy will not be able to maintain the initiative is that his shortage of troops renders it impossible for him to carry on the offensive

indefinitely. Our offensive warfare in campaigns and our guerrilla warfare behind the enemy lines, together with other factors, constitute the second reason why he will have to cease his offensive at a certain limit and will not be able to keep his initiative. The existence of the Soviet Union and changes in the international situation constitute the third reason. Thus it can be seen that the enemy's initiative is limited and can be shattered. If, in military operations, China can keep up offensive warfare by her main forces in campaigns and battles, vigorously develop guerrilla warfare in the enemy's rear and mobilize the people on a broad scale politically, we can gradually build up a position of strategic initiative.

85. Let us now discuss flexibility. What is flexibility? It is the concrete realization of the initiative in military operations; it is the flexible employment of armed forces. The flexible employment of armed forces is the central task in directing a war, a task most difficult to perform well. In addition to organizing and educating the army and the people, the business of war consists in the employment of troops in combat, and all these things are done to win the fight. Of course it is difficult to organize an army, etc., but it is even more difficult to employ it, particularly when the weak are fighting the strong. To do so requires subjective ability of a very high order and requires the overcoming of the confusion, obscurity and uncertainty peculiar to war and the discovery of order, clarity and certainty in it; only thus can flexibility in command be realized.

86. The basic principle of field operations for the War of Resistance Against Japan is quick-decision offensive warfare on exterior lines. There are various tactics or methods for giving effect to this principle, such as dispersion and concentration of forces, diverging advance and converging attack,

the offensive and the defensive, assault and containment, encirclement and outflanking, advance and retreat. It is easy to understand these tactics, but not at all easy to employ and vary them flexibly. Here the three crucial links are the time, the place and the troops. No victory can be won unless the time, the place and the troops are well chosen. For example, in attacking an enemy force on the move, if we strike too early, we expose ourselves and give the enemy a chance to prepare, and if we strike too late, the enemy may have encamped and concentrated his forces, presenting us with a hard nut to crack. This is the question of the time. If we select a point of assault on the left flank which actually turns out to be the enemy's weak point, victory will be easy; but if we select the right flank and hit a snag, nothing will be achieved. This is the question of the place. If a particular unit of our forces is employed for a particular task, victory may be easy; but if another unit is employed for the same task, it may be hard to achieve results. This is the question of the troops. We should know not only how to employ tactics but how to vary them. For flexibility of command the important task is to make changes such as from the offensive to the defensive or from the defensive to the offensive, from advance to retreat or from retreat to advance, from containment to assault or from assault to containment, from encirclement to outflanking or from outflanking to encirclement, and to make such changes properly and in good time according to the circumstances of the troops and terrain on both sides. This is true of command in campaigns and strategic command as well as of command in battles.

87. The ancients said: "Ingenuity in varying tactics depends on mother wit"; this "ingenuity", which is what we mean by flexibility, is the contribution of the intelligent

commander. Flexibility does not mean recklessness; recklessness must be rejected. Flexibility consists in the intelligent
commander's ability to take timely and appropriate measures
on the basis of objective conditions after "judging the hour
and sizing up the situation" (the "situation" includes the
enemy's situation, our situation and the terrain), and this
flexibility is "ingenuity in varying tactics". On the basis of
this ingenuity, we can win more victories in quick-decision
offensive warfare on exterior lines, change the balance of
forces in our favour, gain the initiative over the enemy, and
overwhelm and crush him so that the final victory will be
ours.

88. Let us now discuss the question of planning. Because
of the uncertainty peculiar to war, it is much more difficult
to prosecute war according to plan than is the case with other
activities. Yet, since "preparedness ensures success and unpreparedness spells failure", there can be no victory in war
without advance planning and preparations. There is no
absolute certainty in war, and yet it is not without some
degree of relative certainty. We are comparatively certain
about our own situation. We are very uncertain about the
enemy's, but here too there are signs for us to read, clues to
follow and sequences of phenomena to ponder. These form
what we call a degree of relative certainty, which provides
an objective basis for planning in war. Modern technical
developments (telegraphy, radio, aeroplanes, motor vehicles,
railways, steamships, etc.) have added to the possibilities of
planning in war. However, complete or stable planning is
difficult because there is only very limited and transient
certainty in war; such planning must change with the movement (flow or change) of the war and vary in degree according
to the scale of the war. Tactical plans, such as plans for

attack or defence by small formations or units, often have to be changed several times a day. A plan of campaign, that is, of action by large formations, can generally stand till the conclusion of the campaign, in the course of which, however, it is often changed partially or sometimes even wholly. A strategic plan based on the over-all situation of both belligerents is still more stable, but it too is applicable only in a given strategic stage and has to be changed when the war moves towards a new stage. The making and changing of tactical, campaign and strategic plans in accordance with scope and circumstance is a key factor in directing a war; it is the concrete expression of flexibility in war, in other words, it is also ingenuity in varying one's tactics. Commanders at all levels in the anti-Japanese war should take note.

89. Because of the fluidity of war, some people categorically deny that war plans or policies can be relatively stable, describing such plans or policies as "mechanical". This view is wrong. In the preceding section we fully recognized that, because the circumstances of war are only relatively certain and the flow (movement or change) of war is rapid, war plans or policies can be only relatively stable and have to be changed or revised in good time in accordance with changing circumstances and the flow of the war; otherwise we would become mechanists. But one must not deny the need for war plans or policies that are relatively stable over given periods; to negate this is to negate everything, including the war itself as well as the negator himself. As both military conditions and operations are relatively stable, we must grant the relative stability of the war plans and policies resulting from them. For example, since both the circumstances of the war in northern China and the dispersed nature of the Eighth Route Army's operations are relatively stable

for a particular stage, it is absolutely necessary during this stage to acknowledge the relative stability of the Eighth Route Army's strategic principle of operation, namely, "Guerrilla warfare is basic, but lose no chance for mobile warfare under favourable conditions." The period of validity of a plan for a campaign is shorter than that of a strategic plan, and for a tactical plan it is shorter still, but each is stable over a given period. Anyone denying this point would have no way of handling warfare and would become a relativist in war with no settled views, for whom one course is just as wrong or just as right as another. No one denies that even a plan valid for a given period is fluid; otherwise, one plan would never be abandoned in favour of another. But it is fluid within limits, fluid within the bounds of the various war operations undertaken for carrying it out, but not fluid as to its essence; in other words, it is quantitatively but not qualitatively fluid. Within such a given period of time, this essence is definitely not fluid, which is what we mean by relative stability within a given period. In the great river of absolute fluidity throughout the war there is relative stability at each particular stretch — such is our fundamental view regarding war plans or policies.

90. Having dealt with protracted defensive warfare on interior lines in strategy and with quick-decision offensive warfare on exterior lines in campaigns and battles, and also with the initiative, flexibility and planning, we can now sum up briefly. The anti-Japanese war must have a plan. War plans, which are the concrete application of strategy and tactics, must be flexible so that they can be adapted to the circumstances of the war. We should always seek to transform our inferiority into superiority and our passivity into the initiative so as to change the situation as between the

enemy and ourselves. All these find expression in quick-decision offensive warfare on exterior lines in campaigns and battles and protracted defensive warfare on interior lines in strategy.

## MOBILE WARFARE, GUERRILLA WARFARE AND POSITIONAL WARFARE

91. A war will take the form of mobile warfare when its content is quick-decision offensive warfare on exterior lines in campaigns and battles within the framework of the strategy of interior lines, protracted war and defence. Mobile warfare is the form in which regular armies wage quick-decision offensive campaigns and battles on exterior lines along extensive fronts and over big areas of operation. At the same time, it includes "mobile defence", which is conducted when necessary to facilitate such offensive battles; it also includes positional attack and positional defence in a supplementary role. Its characteristics are regular armies, superiority of forces in campaigns and battles, the offensive, and fluidity.

92. China has a vast territory and an immense number of soldiers, but her troops are inadequately equipped and trained; the enemy's forces, on the other hand, are inadequate in number, but better equipped and trained. In this situation, there is no doubt that we must adopt offensive mobile warfare as our primary form of warfare, supplementing it by others and integrating them all into mobile warfare. We must oppose "only retreat, never advance", which is flightism, and at the same time oppose "only advance, never retreat", which is desperate recklessness.

93. One of the characteristics of mobile warfare is fluidity, which not only permits but requires a field army to advance and to withdraw in great strides. However, it has nothing in common with flightism of the Han Fu-chu brand.[32] The primary requirement of war is to destroy the enemy, and the other requirement is self-preservation. The object of self-preservation is to destroy the enemy, and to destroy the enemy is in turn the most effective means of self-preservation. Hence mobile warfare is in no way an excuse for people like Han Fu-chu and can never mean moving only backward, and never forward; that kind of "moving" which negates the basic offensive character of mobile warfare would, in practice, "move" China out of existence despite her vastness.

94. However, the other view, which we call the desperate recklessness of "only advance, never retreat", is also wrong. The mobile warfare we advocate, the content of which is quick-decision offensive warfare on exterior lines in campaigns and battles, includes positional warfare in a supplementary role, "mobile defence" and retreat, without all of which mobile warfare cannot be fully carried out. Desperate recklessness is military short-sightedness, originating often from fear of losing territory. A man who acts with desperate recklessness does not know that one characteristic of mobile warfare is fluidity, which not only permits but requires a field army to advance and to withdraw in great strides. On the positive side, in order to draw the enemy into a fight unfavourable to him but favourable to us, it is usually necessary that he should be on the move and that we should have a number of advantages, such as favourable terrain, a vulnerable enemy, a local population that can prevent the leakage of information, and the enemy's fatigue and unpreparedness. This requires that the enemy should advance,

and we should not grudge a temporary loss of part of our territory. For the temporary loss of part of our territory is the price we pay for the permanent preservation of all our territory, including the recovery of lost territory. On the negative side, whenever we are forced into a disadvantageous position which fundamentally endangers the preservation of our forces, we should have the courage to retreat, so as to preserve our forces and hit the enemy when new opportunities arise. In their ignorance of this principle, the advocates of desperate action will contest a city or a piece of ground even when the position is obviously and definitely unfavourable; as a result, they not only lose the city or ground but fail to preserve their forces. We have always advocated the policy of "luring the enemy in deep", precisely because it is the most effective military policy for a weak army strategically on the defensive to employ against a strong army.

95. Among the forms of warfare in the anti-Japanese war mobile warfare comes first and guerrilla warfare second. When we say that in the entire war mobile warfare is primary and guerrilla warfare supplementary, we mean that the outcome of the war depends mainly on regular warfare, especially in its mobile form, and that guerrilla warfare cannot shoulder the main responsibility in deciding the outcome. It does not follow, however, that the role of guerrilla warfare is unimportant in the strategy of the war. Its role in the strategy of the war as a whole is second only to that of mobile warfare, for without its support we cannot defeat the enemy. In saying this we also have in mind the strategic task of developing guerrilla warfare into mobile warfare. Guerrilla warfare will not remain the same throughout this long and cruel war, but will rise to a higher level and

develop into mobile warfare. Thus the strategic role of guerrilla warfare is twofold, to support regular warfare and to transform itself into regular warfare. Considering the unprecedented extent and duration of guerrilla warfare in China's War of Resistance, it is all the more important not to underestimate its strategic role. Guerrilla warfare in China, therefore, has not only its tactical but also its peculiar strategic problems. I have already discussed this in *Problems of Strategy in Guerrilla War Against Japan*. As indicated above, the forms of warfare in the three strategic stages of the War of Resistance are as follows. In the first stage mobile warfare is primary, while guerrilla and positional warfare are supplementary. In the second stage guerrilla warfare will advance to the first place and will be supplemented by mobile and positional warfare. In the third stage mobile warfare will again become the primary form and will be supplemented by positional and guerrilla warfare. But the mobile warfare of the third stage will no longer be undertaken solely by the original regular forces; part, possibly quite an important part, will be undertaken by forces which were originally guerrillas but which will have progressed from guerrilla to mobile warfare. From the viewpoint of all three stages in China's War of Resistance Against Japan, guerrilla warfare is definitely indispensable. Our guerrilla war will present a great drama unparalleled in the annals of war. For this reason, out of the millions of China's regular troops, it is absolutely necessary to assign at least several hundred thousand to disperse through all enemy-occupied areas, arouse the masses to arm themselves, and wage guerrilla warfare in co-ordination with the masses. The regular forces so assigned should shoulder this sacred task conscientiously, and they should not think their status lowered because they fight fewer big battles and for the time being do not appear as national heroes. Any such thinking is wrong. Guerrilla warfare does not bring as quick results or as great renown as regular warfare, but "a long road tests a horse's strength and a long task proves a man's heart", and in the course of this long and cruel war guerrilla warfare will demonstrate its immense power; it is indeed no ordinary undertaking. Moreover, such regular forces can conduct guerrilla warfare when dispersed and mobile warfare when concentrated, as the Eighth Route Army has been doing. The principle of the Eighth Route Army is, "Guerrilla warfare is basic, but lose no chance for mobile warfare under favourable conditions." This principle is perfectly correct; the views of its opponents are wrong.

96. At China's present technical level, positional warfare, defensive or offensive, is generally impracticable, and this is where our weakness manifests itself. Moreover, the enemy is also exploiting the vastness of our territory to bypass our fortified positions. Hence positional warfare cannot be an important, still less the principal, means for us. But in the first and second stages of the war, it is possible and essential, within the scope of mobile warfare, to employ localized positional warfare in a supplementary role in campaigns. Semi-positional "mobile defence" is a still more essential part of mobile warfare undertaken for the purpose of resisting the enemy at every step, thereby depleting his forces and gaining extra time. China must strive to increase her supplies of modern weapons so that she can fully carry out the tasks of positional attack in the stage of the strategic counter-offensive. In this third stage positional warfare will undoubtedly play a greater role, for then the enemy will be holding fast to his positions, and we shall not be able to recover our lost

territory unless we launch powerful positional attacks in support of mobile warfare. Nevertheless, in the third stage too, we must exert our every effort to make mobile warfare the primary form of warfare. For the art of directing war and the active role of man are largely nullified in positional warfare such as that fought in Western Europe in the second half of World War I. It is only natural that the war should be taken "out of the trenches", since the war is being fought in the vast expanses of China and since our side will remain poorly equipped technically for quite a long time. Even during the third stage, when China's technical position will be better, she will hardly surpass her enemy in that respect, and so will have to concentrate on highly mobile warfare, without which she cannot achieve final victory. Hence, throughout the War of Resistance China will not adopt positional warfare as primary; the primary or important forms are mobile warfare and guerrilla warfare. These two forms of warfare will afford full play to the art of directing war and to the active role of man — what a piece of good fortune out of our misfortune!

## WAR OF ATTRITION AND WAR OF ANNIHILATION

97. As we have said before, the essence, or the object, of war is to preserve oneself and destroy the enemy. Since there are three forms of warfare, mobile, positional and guerrilla, for achieving this object, and since they differ in degrees of effectiveness, there arises the broad distinction between war of attrition and war of annihilation.

98. To begin with, we may say that the anti-Japanese war is at once a war of attrition and a war of annihilation. Why? Because the enemy is still exploiting his strength and retains strategic superiority and strategic initiative, and therefore, unless we fight campaigns and battles of annihilation, we cannot effectively and speedily reduce his strength and break his superiority and initiative. We still have our weakness and have not yet rid ourselves of strategic inferiority and passivity; therefore, unless we fight campaigns and battles of annihilation, we cannot win time to improve our internal and international situation and alter our unfavourable position. Hence campaigns of annihilation are the means of attaining the objective of strategic attrition. In this sense war of annihilation *is* war of attrition. It is chiefly by using the method of attrition through annihilation that China can wage protracted war.

99. But the objective of strategic attrition may also be achieved by campaigns of attrition. Generally speaking, mobile warfare performs the task of annihilation, positional warfare performs the task of attrition, and guerrilla warfare performs both simultaneously; the three forms of warfare are thus distinguished from one another. In this sense war of annihilation is different from war of attrition. Campaigns of attrition are supplementary but necessary in protracted war.

100. Speaking theoretically and in terms of China's needs, in order to achieve the strategic objective of greatly depleting the enemy's forces, China in her defensive stage should not only exploit the function of annihilation, which is fulfilled primarily by mobile warfare and partially by guerrilla warfare, but also exploit the function of attrition, which is fulfilled primarily by positional warfare (which itself is

supplementary) and partially by guerrilla warfare. In the stage of stalemate we should continue to exploit the functions of annihilation and attrition fulfilled by guerrilla and mobile warfare for further large-scale depletion of the enemy's forces. All this is aimed at protracting the war, gradually changing the general balance of forces and preparing the conditions for our counter-offensive. During the strategic counter-offensive, we should continue to employ the method of attrition through annihilation so as finally to expel the enemy.

101. But as a matter of fact, it was our experience in the last ten months that many or even most of the mobile warfare campaigns became campaigns of attrition, and guerrilla warfare did not adequately fulfil its proper function of annihilation in certain areas. The positive aspect is that at least we depleted the enemy's forces, which is important both for the protracted warfare and for our final victory, and did not shed our blood in vain. But the drawbacks are first, that we did not sufficiently deplete the enemy, and second, that we were unable to avoid rather heavy losses and captured little war booty. Although we should recognize the objective cause of this situation, namely, the disparity between us and the enemy in technical equipment and in the training of troops, in any case it is necessary, both theoretically and practically, to urge that our main forces should fight vigorous battles of annihilation whenever circumstances are favourable. And although our guerrilla units have to wage battles of pure attrition in performing specific tasks such as sabotage and harassment, it is necessary to advocate and vigorously carry out campaigns and battles of annihilation whenever circumstances are favourable, so as greatly to deplete the enemy's forces and greatly replenish our own.

102. The "exterior lines", the "quick-decision" and the "offensive" in quick-decision offensive warfare on exterior lines and the "mobility" in mobile warfare find their main operational expression in the use of encircling and outflanking tactics; hence the necessity for concentrating superior forces. Therefore concentration of forces and the use of encircling and outflanking tactics are the prerequisites for mobile warfare, that is, for quick-decision offensive warfare on exterior lines. All this is aimed at annihilating the enemy forces.

103. The strength of the Japanese army lies not only in its weapons but also in the training of its officers and men — its degree of organization, its self-confidence arising from never having been defeated, its superstitious belief in the Mikado and in supernatural beings, its arrogance, its contempt for the Chinese people and other such characteristics, all of which stem from long years of indoctrination by the Japanese warlords and from the Japanese national tradition. This is the chief reason why we have taken very few prisoners, although we have killed and wounded a great many enemy troops. It is a point that has been underestimated by many people in the past. To destroy these enemy characteristics will be a long process. The first thing to do is to give the matter serious attention, and then patiently and systematically to work at it in the political field and in the fields of international propaganda and the Japanese people's movement; in the military sphere war of annihilation is of course one of the means. In these enemy characteristics pessimists may find a basis for the theory of national subjugation, and passively minded military men a basis for opposition to war of annihilation. We, on the contrary, maintain that these strong points of the Japanese army can be destroyed and that their destruction has already begun. The chief method of destroying

them is to win over the Japanese soldiers politically. We should understand, rather than hurt, their pride and channel it in the proper direction and, by treating prisoners of war leniently, lead the Japanese soldiers to see the anti-popular character of the aggression committed by the Japanese rulers. On the other hand, we should demonstrate to the Japanese soldiers the indomitable spirit and the heroic, stubborn fighting capacity of the Chinese army and the Chinese people, that is, we should deal them blows in battles of annihilation. Our experience in the last ten months of military operations shows that it is possible to annihilate enemy forces — witness the Pinghsingkuan and Taierhchuang campaigns. The Japanese army's morale is beginning to sag, its soldiers do not understand the aim of the war, they are engulfed by the Chinese armies and by the Chinese people, in assault they show far less courage than the Chinese soldiers, and so on; all these are objective factors favourable to waging battles of annihilation, and they will, moreover, steadily develop as the war becomes protracted. From the viewpoint of destroying the enemy's overweening arrogance through battles of annihilation, such battles are one of the prerequisites for shortening the war and accelerating the emancipation of the Japanese soldiers and the Japanese people. Cats make friends with cats, and nowhere in the world do cats make friends with mice.

104. On the other hand, it must be admitted that for the present we are inferior to the enemy in technical equipment and in troop training. Therefore, it is often difficult to achieve the maximum in annihilation, such as capturing the whole or the greater part of an enemy force, especially when fighting on the plains. In this connection the excessive demands of the theorists of quick victory are wrong. What

should be demanded of our forces in the anti-Japanese war is that they should fight battles of annihilation as far as possible. In favourable circumstances, we should concentrate superior forces in every battle and employ encircling and outflanking tactics — encircle part if not all of the enemy forces, capture part if not all of the encircled forces, and inflict heavy casualties on part of the encircled forces if we cannot capture them. In circumstances which are unfavourable for battles of annihilation, we should fight battles of attrition. In favourable circumstances, we should employ the principle of concentration of forces, and in unfavourable circumstances that of their dispersion. As for the relationship of command in campaigns, we should apply the principle of centralized command in the former and that of decentralized command in the latter. These are the basic principles of field operations for the War of Resistance Against Japan.

## THE POSSIBILITIES OF EXPLOITING
## THE ENEMY'S MISTAKES

105. The enemy command itself provides a basis for the possibility of defeating Japan. History has never known an infallible general, and the enemy makes mistakes just as we ourselves can hardly avoid making them; hence, the possibility exists of exploiting the enemy's errors. In the ten months of his war of aggression the enemy has already made many mistakes in strategy and tactics. There are five major ones.

First, piecemeal reinforcement. This is due to the enemy's underestimation of China and also to his shortage of troops. The enemy has always looked down on us.

After grabbing the four northeastern provinces at small cost, he occupied eastern Hopei and northern Chahar, all by way of strategic reconnaissance. The conclusion the enemy came to was that the Chinese nation is a heap of loose sand. Thus, thinking that China would crumble at a single blow, he mapped out a plan of "quick decision", attempting with very small forces to send us scampering in panic. He did not expect to find such great unity and such immense powers of resistance as China has shown during the past ten months, forgetting as he did that China is already in an era of progress and already has an advanced political party, an advanced army and an advanced people. Meeting with setbacks, the enemy then increased his forces piecemeal from about a dozen to thirty divisions. If he wants to advance, he will have to augment his forces still further. But because of Japan's antagonism with the Soviet Union and her inherent shortage of manpower and finances, there are inevitable limits to the maximum number of men she can throw in and to the furthest extent of her advance.

Second, absence of a main direction of attack. Before the Taierhchuang campaign, the enemy had divided his forces more or less evenly between northern and central China and had again divided them inside each of these areas. In northern China, for instance, he divided his forces among the Tientsin-Pukow, the Peiping-Hankow and the Tatung-Puchow Railways, and along each of these lines he suffered some casualties and left some garrisons in the places occupied, after which he lacked the forces for further advances. After the Taierhchuang defeat, from which he learned a lesson, the enemy concentrated his main forces in the direction of Hsuchow, and so temporarily corrected this mistake.

Third, lack of strategic co-ordination. On the whole co-ordination exists within the groups of enemy forces in northern China and in central China, but there is glaring lack of co-ordination between the two. When his forces on the southern section of the Tientsin-Pukow Railway attacked Hsiaopengpu, those on the northern section made no move, and when his forces on the northern section attacked Taierhchuang, those on the southern section made no move. After the enemy came to grief at both places, the Japanese minister of war arrived on an inspection tour and the chief of general staff turned up to take charge, and for the moment, it seemed, there was co-ordination. The landlord class, the bourgeoisie and the warlords of Japan have very serious internal contradictions, which are growing, and the lack of military co-ordination is one of the concrete manifestations of this fact.

Fourth, failure to grasp strategic opportunities. This failure was conspicuously shown in the enemy's halt after the occupation of Nanking and Taiyuan, chiefly because of his shortage of troops and his lack of a strategic pursuit force.

Fifth, encirclement of large, but annihilation of small, numbers. Before the Taierhchuang campaign, in the campaigns of Shanghai, Nanking, Tsangchow, Paoting, Nankow, Hsinkou and Linfen, many Chinese troops were routed but few were taken prisoner, which shows the stupidity of the enemy command.

These five errors — piecemeal reinforcement, absence of a main direction of attack, lack of strategic co-ordination, failure to grasp opportunities, and encirclement of large, but annihilation of small, numbers — were all points of incompetence in the Japanese command before the Taierhchuang campaign. Although the enemy has since made some improvements, he cannot possibly avoid repeating his errors because of his shortage of troops, his internal contradictions and other factors. In addition, what he gains at one point he loses at another. For instance, when he concentrated his forces in northern China on Hsuchow, he left a great vacuum in the occupied areas in northern China, which gave us full scope for developing guerrilla warfare. These mistakes were of the enemy's own making and not induced by us. On our part, we can deliberately make the enemy commit errors, that is, we can mislead him and manoeuvre him into the desired position by ingenious and effective moves with the help of a well-organized local population, for example, by "making a feint to the east but attacking in the west". This possibility has already been discussed. All the above shows that in the enemy's command, too, we can find some basis for victory. Of course, we should not take it as an important basis for our strategic planning; on the contrary, the only reliable course is to base our planning on the assumption that the enemy will make few mistakes. Besides, the enemy can exploit our mistakes just as we can exploit his. It is the duty of our command to allow him the minimum of opportunities for doing so. Actually, the enemy command has committed errors, will again commit errors in the future, and can be made to do so through our endeavours. All these errors we can exploit, and it is the business of our generals in the War of Resistance to do their utmost to seize upon them. However, although much of the enemy's strategic and campaign command is incompetent, there are quite a few excellent points in his battle command, that is, in his unit and small formation tactics, and here we should learn from him.

## THE QUESTION OF DECISIVE ENGAGEMENTS IN THE ANTI-JAPANESE WAR

106. The question of decisive engagements in the anti-Japanese war should be approached from three aspects: we should resolutely fight a decisive engagement in every campaign or battle in which we are sure of victory; we should avoid a decisive engagement in every campaign or battle in which we are not sure of victory; and we should absolutely avoid a strategically decisive engagement on which the fate of the whole nation is staked. The characteristics differentiating our War of Resistance Against Japan from many other wars are also revealed in this question of decisive engagements. In the first and second stages of the war, which are marked by the enemy's strength and our weakness, the enemy's objective is to have us concentrate our main forces for a decisive engagement. Our objective is exactly the opposite. We want to choose conditions favourable to us, concentrate superior forces and fight decisive campaigns or battles only when we are sure of victory, as in the battles at Pinghsingkuan, Taierhchuang and other places; we want to avoid decisive engagements under unfavourable conditions when we are not sure of victory, this being the policy we adopted in the Changteh and other campaigns. As for fighting a strategically decisive engagement on which the fate of the whole nation is staked, we simply must not do so, as witness the recent withdrawal from Hsuchow. The enemy's

plan for a "quick decision" was thus foiled, and now he cannot help fighting a protracted war with us. These principles are impracticable in a country with a small territory, and hardly practicable in a country that is very backward politically. They are practicable in China because she is a big country and is in an era of progress. If strategically decisive engagements are avoided, then "as long as the green mountains are there, one need not worry about firewood", for even though some of our territory may be lost, we shall still have plenty of room for manoeuvre and thus be able to promote and await domestic progress, international support and the internal disintegration of the enemy; that is the best policy for us in the anti-Japanese war. Unable to endure the arduous trials of a protracted war and eager for an early triumph, the impetuous theorists of quick victory clamour for a strategically decisive engagement the moment the situation takes a slightly favourable turn. To do what they want would be to inflict incalculable damage on the entire war, spell finis to the protracted war, and land us in the enemy's deadly trap; actually, it would be the worst policy. Undoubtedly, if we are to avoid decisive engagements, we shall have to abandon territory, and we must have the courage to do so when (and only when) it becomes completely unavoidable. At such times we should not feel the slightest regret, for this policy of trading space for time is correct. History tells us how Russia made a courageous retreat to avoid a decisive engagement and then defeated Napoleon, the terror of his age. Today China should do likewise.

107. Are we not afraid of being denounced as "non-resisters"? No, we are not. Not to fight at all but to compromise with the enemy — that is non-resistance, which

should not only be denounced but must never be tolerated. We must resolutely fight the War of Resistance, but in order to avoid the enemy's deadly trap, it is absolutely necessary that we should not allow our main forces to be finished off at one blow, which would make it difficult to continue the War of Resistance — in brief, it is absolutely necessary to avoid national subjugation. To have doubts on this point is to be short-sighted on the question of the war and is sure to lead one into the ranks of the subjugationists. We have criticized the desperate recklessness of "only advance, never retreat" precisely because, if it became the fashion, this doctrine would make it impossible to continue the War of Resistance and would lead to the danger of ultimate national subjugation.

108. We are for decisive engagements whenever circumstances are favourable, whether in battles or in major or minor campaigns, and in this respect we should never tolerate passivity. Only through such decisive engagements can we achieve the objective of annihilating or depleting the enemy forces, and every soldier in the anti-Japanese war should resolutely play his part. For this purpose considerable partial sacrifices are necessary; to avoid any sacrifice whatsoever is the attitude of cowards and of those afflicted by the fear of Japan and must be firmly opposed. The execution of Li Fu-ying, Han Fu-chu and other flightists was justified. Within the scope of correct war planning, encouraging the spirit and practice of heroic self-sacrifice and dauntless advance in battle is absolutely necessary and inseparable from the waging of protracted war and the achievement of final victory. We have strongly condemned the flightism of "only retreat, never advance" and have supported the strict enforcement of discipline, because it is only through heroic

decisive engagements, fought under a correct plan, that we can vanquish the powerful enemy; flightism, on the contrary, gives direct support to the theory of national subjugation.

109. Is it not self-contradictory to fight heroically first and then abandon territory? Will not our heroic fighters have shed their blood in vain? That is not at all the way questions should be posed. To eat and then to empty your bowels — is this not to eat in vain? To sleep and then to get up — is this not to sleep in vain? Can questions be posed in such a way? I would suppose not. To keep on eating, to keep on sleeping, to keep on fighting heroically all the way to the Yalu River without a stop — these are subjectivist and formalist illusions, not realities of life. As everybody knows, although in fighting and shedding our blood in order to gain time and prepare the counter-offensive we have had to abandon some territory, in fact we have gained time, we have achieved the objective of annihilating and depleting enemy forces, we have acquired experience in fighting, we have aroused hitherto inactive people and improved our international standing. Has our blood been shed in vain? Certainly not. Territory has been given up in order to preserve our military forces and indeed to preserve territory, because if we do not abandon part of our territory when conditions are unfavourable but blindly fight decisive engagements without the least assurance of winning, we shall lose our military forces and then be unable to avoid the loss of all our territory, to say nothing of recovering territory already lost. A capitalist must have capital to run his business, and if he loses it all he is no longer a capitalist. Even a gambler must have money to stake, and if he risks it all on a single throw and his luck fails, he cannot gamble any more. Events have their twists and turns and do not follow a straight line,

and war is no exception; only formalists are unable to comprehend this truth.

110. I think the same will also hold true for the decisive engagements in the stage of strategic counter-offensive. Although by then the enemy will be in the inferior and we in the superior position, the principle of "fighting profitable decisive engagements and avoiding unprofitable ones" will still apply and will continue to apply until we have fought our way to the Yalu River. This is how we will be able to maintain our initiative from beginning to end, and as for the enemy's "challenges" and other people's "taunts", we should imperturbably brush them aside and ignore them. In the War of Resistance only those generals who show this kind of firmness can be deemed courageous and wise. This is beyond the ken of those who "jump whenever touched". Even though we are in a more or less passive position strategically in this first stage of the war, we should have the initiative in every campaign; and of course we should have the initiative throughout the later stages. We are for protracted war and final victory, we are not gamblers who risk everything on a single throw.


## THE ARMY AND THE PEOPLE ARE
## THE FOUNDATION OF VICTORY

111. Japanese imperialism will never relax in its aggression against and repression of revolutionary China; this is determined by its imperialist nature. If China did not resist, Japan would easily seize all China without firing a single shot, as she did the four northeastern provinces. Since China is resisting, it is an inexorable law that Japan will try

to repress this resistance until the force of her repression is exceeded by the force of China's resistance. The Japanese landlord class and bourgeoisie are very ambitious, and in order to drive south to Southeast Asia and north to Siberia, they have adopted the policy of breaking through in the centre by first attacking China. Those who think that Japan will know where to stop and be content with the occupation of northern China and of Kiangsu and Chekiang Provinces completely fail to perceive that imperialist Japan, which has developed to a new stage and is approaching extinction, differs from the Japan of the past. When we say that there is a definite limit both to the number of men Japan can throw in and to the extent of her advance, we mean that with her available strength, Japan can only commit part of her forces against China and only penetrate China as far as their capacity allows, for she also wants to attack in other directions and has to defend herself against other enemies; at the same time China has given proof of progress and capacity for stubborn resistance, and it is inconceivable that there should be fierce attacks by Japan without inevitable resistance by China. Japan cannot occupy the whole of China, but she will spare no effort to suppress China's resistance in all the areas she can reach, and will not stop until internal and external developments push Japanese imperialism to the brink of the grave. There are only two possible outcomes to the political situation in Japan. Either the downfall of her entire ruling class occurs rapidly, political power passes to the people and war thus comes to an end, which is impossible at the moment; or her landlord class and bourgeoisie become more and more fascist and maintain the war until the day of their downfall, which is the very road Japan is now travelling. There can be no other outcome.

Those who hope that the moderates among the Japanese bourgeoisie will come forward and stop the war are only harbouring illusions. The reality of Japanese politics for many years has been that the bourgeois moderates of Japan have fallen captive to the landlords and the financial magnates. Now that Japan has launched war against China, so long as she does not suffer a fatal blow from Chinese resistance and still retains sufficient strength, she is bound to attack Southeast Asia or Siberia, or even both. She will do so once war breaks out in Europe; in their wishful calculations, the rulers of Japan have it worked out on a grandiose scale. Of course, it is possible that Japan will have to drop her original plan of invading Siberia and adopt a mainly defensive attitude towards the Soviet Union on account of Soviet strength and of the serious extent to which Japan herself has been weakened by her war against China. But in that case, so far from relaxing her aggression against China she will intensify it, because then the only way left to her will be to gobble up the weak. China's task of persevering in the War of Resistance, the united front and the protracted war will then become all the more weighty, and it will be all the more necessary not to slacken our efforts in the slightest.

112. Under the circumstances the main prerequisites for China's victory over Japan are nation-wide unity and all-round progress on a scale ten or even a hundred times greater than in the past. China is already in an era of progress and has achieved a splendid unity, but her progress and unity are still far from adequate. That Japan has occupied such an extensive area is due not only to her strength but also to China's weakness; this weakness is entirely the cumulative effect of the various historical errors of the last hundred

years, and especially of the last ten years, which have confined progress to its present bounds. It is impossible to vanquish so strong an enemy without making an extensive and long-term effort. There are many things we have to exert ourselves to do; here I will deal only with two fundamental aspects, the progress of the army and the progress of the people.

113. The reform of our military system requires its modernization and improved technical equipment, without which we cannot drive the enemy back across the Yalu River. In our employment of troops we need progressive, flexible strategy and tactics, without which we likewise cannot win victory. Nevertheless, soldiers are the foundation of an army; unless they are imbued with a progressive political spirit, and unless such a spirit is fostered through progressive political work, it will be impossible to achieve genuine unity between officers and men, impossible to arouse their enthusiasm for the War of Resistance to the full, and impossible to provide a sound basis for the most effective use of all our technical equipment and tactics. When we say that Japan will finally be defeated despite her technical superiority, we mean that the blows we deliver through annihilation and attrition, apart from inflicting losses, will eventually shake the morale of the enemy army whose weapons are not in the hands of politically conscious soldiers. With us, on the contrary, officers and men are at one on the political aim of the War of Resistance. This gives us the foundation for political work among all the anti-Japanese forces. A proper measure of democracy should be put into effect in the army, chiefly by abolishing the feudal practice of bullying and beating and by having officers and men share weal and woe. Once this is done, unity will be achieved between officers and

men, the combat effectiveness of the army will be greatly increased, and there will be no doubt of our ability to sustain the long, cruel war.

114. The richest source of power to wage war lies in the masses of the people. It is mainly because of the unorganized state of the Chinese masses that Japan dares to bully us. When this defect is remedied, then the Japanese aggressor, like a mad bull crashing into a ring of flames, will be surrounded by hundreds of millions of our people standing upright, the mere sound of their voices will strike terror into him, and he will be burned to death. China's armies must have an uninterrupted flow of reinforcements, and the abuses of press-ganging and of buying substitutes,[33] which now exist at the lower levels, must immediately be banned and replaced by widespread and enthusiastic political mobilization, which will make it easy to enlist millions of men. We now have great difficulties in raising money for the war, but once the people are mobilized, finances too will cease to be a problem. Why should a country as large and populous as China suffer from lack of funds? The army must become one with the people so that they see it as their own army. Such an army will be invincible, and an imperialist power like Japan will be no match for it.

115. Many people think that it is wrong methods that make for strained relations between officers and men and between the army and the people, but I always tell them that it is a question of basic attitude (or basic principle), of having respect for the soldiers and the people. It is from this attitude that the various policies, methods and forms ensue. If we depart from this attitude, then the policies, methods and forms will certainly be wrong, and the relations between officers and men and between the army and the people are

bound to be unsatisfactory. Our three major principles for the army's political work are, first, unity between officers and men; second, unity between the army and the people; and third, the disintegration of the enemy forces. To apply these principles effectively, we must start with this basic attitude of respect for the soldiers and the people, and of respect for the human dignity of prisoners of war once they have laid down their arms. Those who take all this as a technical matter and not one of basic attitude are indeed wrong, and they should correct their view.

116. At this moment when the defence of Wuhan and other places has become urgent, it is a task of the utmost importance to arouse the initiative and enthusiasm of the whole army and the whole people to the full in support of the war. There is no doubt that the task of defending Wuhan and other places must be seriously posed and seriously performed. But whether we can be certain of holding them depends not on our subjective desires but on concrete conditions. Among the most important of these conditions is the political mobilization of the whole army and people for the struggle. If a strenuous effort is not made to secure all the necessary conditions, indeed even if one of these conditions is missing, disasters like the loss of Nanking and other places are bound to be repeated. China will have her Madrids in places where the conditions are present. So far China has not had a Madrid, and from now on we should work hard to create several, but it all depends on the conditions. The most fundamental of these is extensive political mobilization of the whole army and people.

117. In all our work we must persevere in the Anti-Japanese National United Front as the general policy. For only with this policy can we persevere in the War of Resistance

and in protracted warfare, bring about a widespread and profound improvement in the relations between officers and men and between the army and the people, arouse to the full the initiative and enthusiasm of the entire army and the entire people in the fight for the defence of all the territory still in our hands and for the recovery of what we have lost, and so win final victory.

118. This question of the political mobilization of the army and the people is indeed of the greatest importance. We have dwelt on it at the risk of repetition precisely because victory is impossible without it. There are, of course, many other conditions indispensable to victory, but political mobilization is the most fundamental. The Anti-Japanese National United Front is a united front of the whole army and the whole people, it is certainly not a united front merely of the headquarters and members of a few political parties; our basic objective in initiating the Anti-Japanese National United Front is to mobilize the whole army and the whole people to participate in it.

## CONCLUSIONS

119. What are our conclusions? They are:

"Under what conditions do you think China can defeat and destroy the forces of Japan?" "Three conditions are required: first, the establishment of an anti-Japanese united front in China; second, the formation of an international anti-Japanese united front; third, the rise of the revolutionary movement of the people in Japan and the Japanese colonies. From the standpoint of the Chinese people, the unity of the people of China is the most important of the three conditions."

"How long do you think such a war would last?" "That depends on the strength of China's anti-Japanese united front and many other conditioning factors involving China and Japan."

"If these conditions are not realized quickly, the war will be prolonged. But in the end, just the same, Japan will certainly be defeated and China will certainly be victorious. Only the sacrifices will be great and there will be a very painful period."

"Our strategy should be to employ our main forces to operate over an extended and fluid front. To achieve success, the Chinese troops must conduct their warfare with a high degree of mobility on extensive battlefields."

"Besides employing trained armies to carry on mobile warfare, we must organize great numbers of guerrilla units among the peasants."

"In the course of the war, China will be able to . . . reinforce the equipment of her troops gradually. Therefore China will be able to conduct positional warfare in the latter period of the war and make positional attacks on the Japanese-occupied areas. Thus Japan's economy will crack under the strain of China's long resistance and the morale of the Japanese forces will break under the trial of innumerable battles. On the Chinese side, however, the growing latent power of resistance will be constantly brought into play and large numbers of revolutionary people will be pouring into the front lines to fight for their freedom. The combination of all these and other factors will enable us to make the final and decisive attacks on the fortifications and bases in the Japanese-occupied areas and

drive the Japanese forces of aggression out of China."
(From an interview with Edgar Snow in July 1936.)

"Thus a new stage has opened in China's political situation. . . . In the present stage the central task is to mobilize all the nation's forces for victory in the War of Resistance."

"The key to victory in the war now lies in developing the resistance that has already begun into a war of total resistance by the whole nation. Only through such a war of total resistance can final victory be won."

"The existence of serious weaknesses in the War of Resistance may lead to setbacks, retreats, internal splits, betrayals, temporary and partial compromises and other such reverses. Therefore it should be realized that the war will be arduous and protracted. But we are confident that, through the efforts of our Party and the whole people, the resistance already started will sweep aside all obstacles and continue to advance and develop." ("Resolution on the Present Situation and the Tasks of the Party", adopted by the Central Committee of the Communist Party of China, August 1937.)

These are our conclusions. In the eyes of the subjugationists the enemy are supermen and we Chinese are worthless, while in the eyes of the theorists of quick victory we Chinese are supermen and the enemy are worthless. Both are wrong. We take a different view; the War of Resistance Against Japan is a protracted war, and the final victory will be China's. These are our conclusions.

120. My lectures end here. The great War of Resistance Against Japan is unfolding, and many people are hoping for a summary of experience to facilitate the winning of complete

victory. What I have discussed is simply the general experience of the past ten months, and it may perhaps serve as a kind of summary. The problem of protracted war deserves wide attention and discussion; what I have given is only an outline, which I hope you will examine and discuss, amend and amplify.


## NOTES

[1] This theory of national subjugation was the view held by the Kuomintang. The Kuomintang was unwilling to resist Japan and fought Japan only under compulsion. After the Lukouchiao Incident (July 7, 1937), the Chiang Kai-shek clique reluctantly took part in the War of Resistance, while the Wang Ching-wei clique became the representatives of the theory of national subjugation, was ready to capitulate to Japan and in fact subsequently did so. However, the idea of national subjugation not only existed in the Kuomintang, but also affected certain sections of the middle strata of society and even certain backward elements among the labouring people. As the corrupt and impotent Kuomintang government lost one battle after another and the Japanese troops advanced unchecked to the vicinity of Wuhan in the first year of the War of Resistance, some backward people became profoundly pessimistic.

[2] These views were to be found within the Communist Party. During the first six months of the War of Resistance, there was a tendency to take the enemy lightly among some members of the Party, who held the view that Japan could be defeated at a single blow. It was not that they felt our own forces to be so strong, since they well knew that the troops and the organized people's forces led by the Communist Party were still small, but that the Kuomintang had begun to resist Japan. In their opinion, the Kuomintang was quite powerful, and, in co-ordination with the Communist Party, could deal Japan telling blows. They made this erroneous appraisal because they saw only one aspect of the Kuomintang, that it was resisting Japan, but overlooked the other aspect, that it was reactionary and corrupt.

[3] Such was the view of Chiang Kai-shek and company. Though they were compelled to resist Japan, Chiang Kai-shek and the Kuomintang pinned their hopes solely on prompt foreign aid and had no confidence in their own strength, much less in the strength of the people.

[4] Taierhchuang is a town in southern Shantung where the Chinese army fought a battle in March 1938 against the Japanese invaders. By pitting 400,000 men against Japan's 70,000 to 80,000, the Chinese army defeated the Japanese.

[5] This view was put forward in an editorial in the *Ta Kung Pao*, then the organ of the Political Science Group in the Kuomintang. Indulging in wishful thinking, this clique hoped that a few more victories of the Taierhchuang type would stop Japan's advance and that there would be no need to mobilize the people for a protracted war, which would threaten the security of its own class. This wishful thinking then pervaded the Kuomintang as a whole.

[6] For many decades, beginning with the end of the 18th century, Britain exported an increasing quantity of opium to China. This traffic not only subjected the Chinese people to drugging but also plundered China of her silver. It aroused fierce opposition in China. In 1840, under the pretext of safeguarding its trade with China, Britain launched armed aggression against her. The Chinese troops led by Lin Tse-hsu put up resistance, and the people in Canton spontaneously organized the "Quell-the-British Corps", which dealt serious blows to the British forces of aggression. In 1842, however, the corrupt Ching regime signed the Treaty of Nanking with the British aggressor. This treaty provided for the payment of indemnities and the cession of Hongkong to Britain, and stipulated that Shanghai, Foochow, Amoy, Ningpo and Canton were to be opened to British trade and that tariff rates for British goods imported into China were to be jointly fixed by China and Britain.

[7] The Taiping Revolution, or the Movement of the Taiping Heavenly Kingdom, was the mid-19th century revolutionary peasant movement against the feudal rule and national oppression of the Ching Dynasty. In January 1851 Hung Hsiu-chuan, Yang Hsiu-ching and other leaders launched an uprising in Chintien Village in Kueiping County, Kwangsi Province, and proclaimed the founding of the Taiping Heavenly Kingdom. Proceeding northward from Kwangsi, their peasant army attacked and occupied Hunan and Hupeh in 1852. In 1853 it marched through Kiangsi and Anhwei and captured Nanking. A section of the forces then continued the drive north and pushed on to the vicinity of Tientsin. However, the Taiping army

failed to build stable base areas in the places it occupied; moreover, after establishing its capital in Nanking, its leading group committed many political and military errors. Therefore it was unable to withstand the combined onslaughts of the counter-revolutionary forces of the Ching government and the British, U.S. and French aggressors, and was finally defeated in 1864.

[8] The Reform Movement of 1898, whose leading spirits were Kang Yu-wei, Liang Chi-chao and Tan Szu-tung, represented the interests of the liberal bourgeoisie and the enlightened landlords. The movement was favoured and supported by Emperor Kuang Hsu, but had no mass basis. Yuan Shih-kai, who had an army behind him, betrayed the reformers to Empress Dowager Tzu Hsi, the leader of the die-hards, who seized power again and had Emperor Kuang Hsu imprisoned and Tan Szu-tung and five others beheaded. Thus the movement ended in tragic defeat.

[9] The Revolution of 1911 was the bourgeois revolution which overthrew the autocratic regime of the Ching Dynasty. On October 10 of that year, a section of the Ching Dynasty's New Army who were under revolutionary influence staged an uprising in Wuchang, Hupeh Province. The existing bourgeois and petty-bourgeois revolutionary societies and the broad masses of the workers, peasants and soldiers responded enthusiastically, and very soon the rule of the Ching Dynasty crumbled. In January 1912, the Provisional Government of the Republic of China was set up in Nanking, with Sun Yat-sen as the Provisional President. Thus China's feudal monarchic system which had lasted for more than two thousand years was brought to an end. The idea of a democratic republic had entered deep in the hearts of the people. But the bourgeoisie which led the revolution was strongly conciliationist in nature. It did not mobilize the peasant masses on an extensive scale to crush the feudal rule of the landlord class in the countryside, but instead handed state power over to the Northern warlord Yuan Shih-kai under imperialist and feudal pressure. As a result, the revolution ended in defeat.

[10] The Northern Expedition was the punitive war against the Northern warlords launched by the revolutionary army which marched north from Kwangtung Province in May-July 1926. The Northern Expeditionary Army, with the Communist Party of China taking part in its leadership and under the Party's influence (the political work in the army was at that time mostly under the charge of Communist Party members), gained the warm support of the broad masses of workers and peasants. In the second half of 1926 and the first half of 1927 it occupied most of the provinces along the Yangtse and Yellow Rivers and defeated the Northern

warlords. In April 1927 this revolutionary war failed as a result of betrayal by the reactionary clique under Chiang Kai-shek within the revolutionary army.

[11] On January 16, 1938, the Japanese cabinet declared in a policy statement that Japan would subjugate China by force. At the same time it tried by threats and blandishments to make the Kuomintang government capitulate, declaring that if the Kuomintang government "continued to plan resistance", the Japanese government would foster a new puppet regime in China and no longer accept the Kuomintang as "the other party" in negotiations.

[12] The capitalists referred to here are chiefly those of the United States.

[13] By "their governments" Comrade Mao Tse-tung is here referring to the governments of the imperialist countries — Britain, the United States and France.

[14] Comrade Mao Tse-tung's prediction that there would be an upswing in China during the stage of stalemate in the War of Resistance Against Japan was completely confirmed in the case of the Liberated Areas under the leadership of the Chinese Communist Party. But there was actually a decline instead of an upswing in the Kuomintang areas, because the ruling clique headed by Chiang Kai-shek was passive in resisting Japan and active in opposing the Communist Party and the people. This roused opposition among the broad masses of the people and raised their political consciousness.

[15] According to the theory that "weapons decide everything", China which was inferior to Japan in regard to arms was bound to be defeated in the war. This view was current among all the leaders of the Kuomintang reaction, Chiang Kai-shek included.

[16] *Weichi* is an old Chinese game, in which the two players try to encircle each other's pieces on the board. When a player's pieces are encircled, they are counted as "dead" (captured). But if there is a sufficient number of blank spaces among the encircled pieces, then the latter are still "alive" (not captured).

[17] Sun Wu-kung is the monkey king in the Chinese novel *Hsi Yu Chi (Pilgrimage to the West)*, written in the 16th century. He could cover 108,000 *li* by turning a somersault. Yet once in the palm of the Buddha, he could not escape from it, however many somersaults he turned. With a flick of his palm Buddha transformed his fingers into the five-peak Mountain of Five Elements, and buried Sun Wu-kung.

[18] *"Fascism is unbridled chauvinism and predatory war,"* said Comrade Georgi Dimitrov in his report to the Seventh World Congress of the Communist International in August 1935, entitled "The Fascist Offensive and the Tasks of the Communist International" (see *Selected Articles and Speeches*, Eng. ed., Lawrence & Wishart, London, 1951, p. 44). In July 1937, Comrade Dimitrov published an article entitled *Fascism Is War*.

[19] V. I. Lenin, *Socialism and War*, Eng. ed., FLPH, Moscow, 1950, p. 19.

[20] *Sun Tzu*, Chapter 3, "The Strategy of Attack".

[21] Chengpu, situated in the southwest of the present Chuancheng County in Shantung Province, was the scene of a great battle between the states of Tsin and Chu in 632 B.C. At the beginning of the battle the Chu troops got the upper hand. The Tsin troops, after making a retreat of 90 *li*, chose the right and left flanks of the Chu troops, their weak spots, and inflicted heavy defeats on them.

[22] The ancient town of Chengkao, in the northwest of the present Chengkao County, Honan Province, was of great military importance. It was the scene of battles fought in 203 B.C. between Liu Pang, King of Han, and Hsiang Yu, King of Chu. At first Hsiang Yu captured Hsingyang and Chengkao and Liu Pang's troops were almost routed. Liu Pang waited until the opportune moment when Hsiang Yu's troops were in midstream crossing the Szeshui River, and then crushed them and recaptured Chengkao.

[23] In 204 B.C., Han Hsin, a general of the state of Han, led his men in a big battle with Chao Hsieh at Chinghsing. Chao Hsieh's army, said to be 200,000 strong, was several times that of Han. Deploying his troops with their backs to a river, Han Hsin led them in valiant combat, and at the same time dispatched some units to attack and occupy the enemy's weakly garrisoned rear. Caught in a pincer, Chao Hsieh's troops were utterly defeated.

[24] The ancient town of Kunyang, in the north of the present Yehhsien County, Honan Province, was the place where Liu Hsiu, founder of the Eastern Han Dynasty, defeated the troops of Wang Mang, Emperor of the Hsin Dynasty, in A.D. 23. There was a huge numerical disparity between the two sides, Liu Hsiu's forces totalling 8,000 to 9,000 men as against Wang Mang's 400,000. But taking advantage of the negligence of Wang Mang's generals, Wang Hsun and Wang Yi, who underestimated the enemy, Liu Hsiu with only three thousand picked troops put Wang Mang's main forces to rout. He followed up this victory by crushing the rest of the enemy troops.

[25] Kuantu was in the northeast of the present Chungmou County, Honan Province, and the scene of the battle between the armies of Tsao Tsao and Yuan Shao in A.D. 200. Yuan Shao had an army of 100,000, while Tsao Tsao had only a meagre force and was short of supplies. Taking advantage of the lack of vigilance on the part of Yuan Shao's troops, who belittled the enemy, Tsao Tsao dispatched his light-footed soldiers to spring a surprise attack on them and set their supplies on fire. Yuan Shao's army was thrown into confusion and its main force wiped out.

[26] The state of Wu was ruled by Sun Chuan, and the state of Wei by Tsao Tsao. Chihpi is situated on the south bank of the Yangtse River, to the northeast of Chiayu, Hupeh Province. In A.D. 208 Tsao Tsao led an army of over 500,000 men, which he proclaimed to be 800,000 strong, to launch an attack on Sun Chuan. The latter, in alliance with Tsao Tsao's antagonist Liu Pei, mustered a force of 30,000. Knowing that Tsao Tsao's army was plagued by epidemics and was unaccustomed to action afloat, the allied forces of Sun Chuan and Liu Pei set fire to Tsao Tsao's fleet and crushed his army.

[27] Yiling, to the east of the present Ichang, Hupeh Province, was the place where Lu Sun, a general of the state of Wu, defeated the army of Liu Pei, ruler of Shu, in A.D. 222. Liu Pei's troops scored successive victories at the beginning of the war and penetrated five or six hundred *li* into the territory of Wu as far as Yiling. Lu Sun, who was defending Yiling, avoided battle for over seven months until Liu Pei "was at his wits' end and his troops were exhausted and demoralized". Then he crushed Liu Pei's troops by taking advantage of a favourable wind to set fire to their tents.

[28] Hsieh Hsuan, a general of Eastern Tsin Dynasty, defeated Fu Chien, ruler of the state of Chin, in A.D. 383 at the Feishui River in Anhwei Province. Fu Chien had an infantry force of more than 600,000, a cavalry force of 270,000 and a guards corps of more than 30,000, while the land and river forces of Eastern Tsin numbered only 80,000. When the armies lined up on opposite banks of the Feishui River, Hsieh Hsuan, taking advantage of the overconfidence and conceit of the enemy troops, requested Fu Chien to move his troops back so as to leave room for the Eastern Tsin troops to cross the river and fight it out. Fu Chien complied, but when he ordered withdrawal, his troops got into a panic and could not be stopped. Seizing the opportunity, the Eastern Tsin troops crossed the river, launched an offensive and crushed the enemy.

[29] In A.D. 383, Fu Chien, the ruler of the state of Chin, belittled the forces of Tsin and attacked them. The Tsin troops defeated the enemy's

advance units at Lochien, Shouyang County, Anhwei Province, and pushed forward by land and water. Ascending the city wall of Shouyang, Fu Chien observed the excellent alignment of the Tsin troops and, mistaking the woods and bushes on Mount Pakung for enemy soldiers, was frightened by the enemy's apparent strength.

[30] Comrade Mao Tse-tung is here referring to the fact that Chiang Kai-shek and Wang Ching-wei, having betrayed the first national democratic united front of the Kuomintang and the Communist Party in 1927, launched a ten-year war against the people, and thus made it impossible for the Chinese people to be organized on a large scale. For this the Kuomintang reactionaries headed by Chiang Kai-shek must be held responsible.

[31] Duke Hsiang of Sung ruled in the Spring and Autumn Era. In 638 B.C., the state of Sung fought with the powerful state of Chu. The Sung forces were already deployed in battle positions when the Chu troops were crossing the river. One of the Sung officers suggested that, as the Chu troops were numerically stronger, this was the moment for attack. But the Duke said, "No, a gentleman should never attack one who is unprepared." When the Chu troops had crossed the river but had not yet completed their battle alignment, the officer again proposed an immediate attack, and once again the Duke said, "No, a gentleman should never attack an army which has not yet completed its battle alignment." The Duke gave the order for attack only after the Chu troops were fully prepared. As a result, the Sung troops met with a disastrous defeat and the Duke himself was wounded.

[32] Han Fu-chu, a Kuomintang warlord, was for several years governor of Shantung. When the Japanese invaders thrust southward to Shantung along the Tientsin-Pukow Railway after occupying Peiping and Tientsin in 1937, Han Fu-chu fled all the way from Shantung to Honan without fighting a single battle.

[33] The Kuomintang expanded its army by press-ganging. Its military and police seized people everywhere, roping them up and treating them like convicts. Those who had money would bribe the Kuomintang officials or pay for substitutes.